Simon &
Becky

mcs

2016

Sorry Darling, It's Way Past Time

An Autobiography by
Thomas Bunn, known as Bunny Thomas

Inspired by Sarah-Jane Szikora and
Vivien McNally.

Dedicated to the memory of Dennis
Docherty.

Sorry Darling, It's Way Past Time

by

Thomas Bunn

ISBN: 978-0-9568074-1-0

This book is published by Thomas Bunn in conjunction with Writersworld Limited and is available to order from most bookshops and Internet book retailers throughout the United Kingdom.

Copy edited by Ian Large

Cover design by Simon Potter

Original cover art by Sarah-Jane Szikora entitled 'Farewell to Dennis'

Printed and bound by www.printondemand-worldwide.com

www.writersworld.co.uk

WRITERSWORLD
2 Bear Close
Woodstock
Oxfordshire
OX20 1JX
England

The text pages of this book are produced via an independent certification process than ensures the trees from which the paper is produced come from well-managed sources that exclude the risk of using illegally logged timber while leaving options to use post-consumer recycled paper as well.

INTRODUCTION

A life is something you have to live before you can write about it. I am no instant celebrity of popular youth culture nor a highly paid artist. The only good reason for penning my story, besides ego, possible financial gain or to stay in the public eye for an extra ten minutes, is that on the day of one's funeral, some synopsis of it could be extracted from its content to pepper up the event and offer a few dubious facts. With luck, it may turn a miserable, sad day into a true celebration.

It can be also help one's own failing memory as time goes on, especially if some progressive carer would bother to use such information as reality orientation and interact with us old and bent. It would be a therapeutic method of generating some response rather than allowing us to sit in a seat, immobile, dreading that moment when a big accident is about to happen and we no longer remember what we have to do.

The biggest change of this life came when Dennis, my lifetime companion and partner of 36 years, left the earthly world after a life of devotion and hard work. He gave unconditional love but at the end developed lung cancer, with some friends saying that I had killed him with 36 years of high hysterics and demands!

Thank goodness for those few friends who knew us well because we can talk, cry and laugh at the realities of our memories and my true life with him. Dennis died on 7th January 2005 but is with me forever; I know it.

*****

CHAPTER 1

It was early one evening when a shaft of light poured unusually through my bedroom window. A film was about start. It was titled, '*Sleepers*'. I knew nothing about it and I called out to Dennis to come and watch it with me. He was not a great watcher of films but once into one he would be as engrossed as I would.

Dennis was in a stage of semi-retirement now, having worked all his life since leaving the Father Hudson's homes many decades before. The film was about to start. If you are unfamiliar with its storyline, it is about a group of young men and their experiences of a catholic institution, now focusing on their adult lives. He was gripped and so was I.

After around half an hour into its story Dennis began, most uncharacteristically, to break down in deep emotional sobs. In 30 years of knowing him I had never seen such an emotional display of cascading raw emotion from him. I kept silent and just held him, sobbing like a beaten child. I remained silent and quietly acknowledged his pain, telling him to let it out. I asked no questions; I knew what was happening to him and I was caught up and blessed to have witnessed this internal explosion.

By this time, Dennis had over the last year sent out hundreds of CVs and filled in dozens and dozens of job application forms, but to no avail. He was too 'experienced', despite his total acceptance of his situation and could have tackled any opportunity given to him. His self-esteem was at an all time low. He was doing some catering from home for a few people and looking after me like a queen.

This human wreckage lying on the bed next to me, propped up by the pillows that I had now placed in the sit-up position, interspersed with silences and gasps for breath, began to explain what was happening. I didn't rush him - for once I was useful. I told him there was no pressure but he needed to get it out and relate it. In his own time.

He began relating a graphic picture of an incident where, one day, a nun beat him so badly the marks on his body were red and some bruises evident. His face was swollen but he just carried on as normal. Suddenly, two 'kind' nuns came to him and said he must go to bed and rest. Dennis, this little boy of possibly six or seven, had asked to see the monsignor who was visiting the excited children of the home - an event they looked forward to. It didn't occur to Dennis at that age that his injuries could not be displayed to this eminent representative of the holy Catholic Church.

He was hidden away in the sick bay and far away from intrusive eyes. No visitor would be aware of his predicament. Not many of those kids had anyone to advocate for them in the early- and mid-1940s. Dennis duly did as he was told and was kept prisoner until the priest had disappeared from yet another one of those boys' home run by these 'angels of mercy' in the name of God. This was just one experience, just another normal frame of reference for him, as it was for many other victims of these cold institutions of mercy.

After a calmer moment and some silences, I was determined to extract more from him. He did eventually, after some tactful coaxing, open up more. He described one day in his early teens (he couldn't remember his exact age) when he was chased in the grounds by much older boys who gave him a few kicks and hurled abuse. They took him behind a copse of trees, ripped his clothes and raped him. He had never ever, at any time, told me of any of this deeply compartmentalised memory that had flown to his conscious mind after years of repressed hard work, either consciously or unconsciously dealt with.

It is amazing that there are experts who say that those abused often turn out to become abusers themselves. This could not be further from the truth in Dennis's case. He abhorred violence, would not endure conflict, nor would he ever raise his hand to anyone. He was gentle, often abrupt yes, but never ever abusive in any outward way. His mutilation came from his own depressive realities turned inward onto himself alone. He suffered by his own hands, not anyone else. In this last decade, I made it my case to look after him and protect him as best I could. Well that was my plan.

I will return to life with Dennis as these writings unfold as I jump from one mindset to another. The times in showbiz will unravel, as will my career in the health service.

*****

My beginnings were forged in the early years of the 1950s in West Bromwich, having been adopted, although I did not discover this for a while. They were a good couple, Hannah and Harold.

Hannah was to live until my eighth year when I was to find her comatose. She had not woken me for school as usual and, even at eight, you sense something is out of order if you have some order in your life. So of course, I went in search of her, believing perhaps she was downstairs and just forgotten or that she had overran her schedule.

Returning upstairs I entered her bedroom. She looked peaceful to me as an eight-year old. At this age I was easily able to lift myself onto the bed. I shook her gently, looking in at her closed eyes, begging her to wake out of this state but to no avail. What a lovely little pale and blue face I thought, as the life had seeped out of her. Death then didn't serve to frighten me witless, but somehow it took on a strange state of grace and almost calmness.

I must have eventually sped out to the rear garden and called the neighbour on the right-side of the house, Mrs Bell a first generation Jamaican living next to us. As I used to play in the entry with their little daughter, it seemed the thing to do. I don't recall so clearly now but she must have launched herself over the wall. Suddenly she was taking me to the neighbour on the other side to be quickly taken to school; it was all hush now.

On return from a bewildering morning at school and strange sympathetic looks from others I was collected by Mrs Ingram who took me in and told me, "Your mother has gone to Jesus." Perhaps she was popping back then.

Harold was, what seemed to me, a quiet, insular man. From that day anyway it became more apparent, as now my eyes were on him. I didn't spend much time with him - how can you when he was out working as all fathers did in those days? A veteran and rare survivor of the Dieppe Raid in France in the Second World War, he was captured by those German chaps and eventually sent to a prisoner of war camp after his injuries had been patched up, from where he eventually was to escape. More on that later.

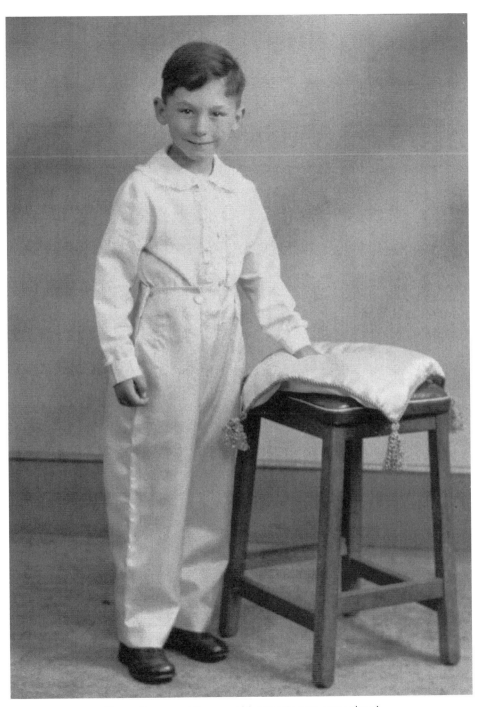

The author aged 5 years old. Dressing up even then!

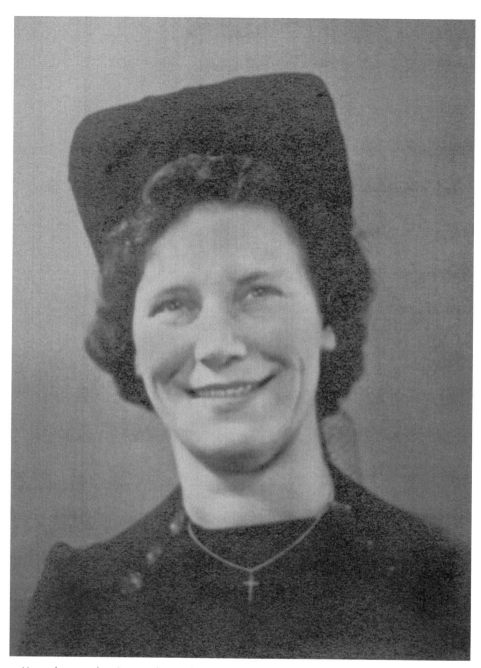

Hannah, my adoptive mother, taken during the war years. She was kind and gentle.

Harold, my adoptive father. He seemed cold and distant but he had his own pain.

I am Bunny Thomas Cabaret, 1970s.

Harold seemed difficult, deep and dark from then on, yet practical and sensible and a very hard-working man. Those few months were the start of a dismal phase but always an interesting one. Sitting in evening silences was the worst, not talking with this lone adult before me and nothing imparted to me from him. It must have been very hard for him.

Nine months after Hannah's death, Harold married her niece, yes Hannah's brother's daughter, in effect my cousin Edith. There seemed a huge age gap between them and, even to me this liaison and arrangement seemed a little confusing and odd. Especially when he told me the day he was going to ask her. I would be in the back seat of his old Morris 8 series E, which only came out for special occasions after cranking up the engine with the magic wand that poked into the engine front of this now vintage number. Well it made a change from his old 1936 Austin Ruby that had been exchanged for this glamour model.

My idealisation of my mother by whom I had just been abandoned was real enough to me and perhaps always stays lurking around in the subconscious. I recall Hannah being soft-spoken, older than most mothers, with a certain refined glamour wearing swagger coats, hats, gloves, heeled shoes and very light make up - never too heavy. I was shocked and sad that she had left me with little explanation and not much discussion by Harold. How do you or I at eight understand such circumstances? Besides, I was convinced that she was an actress! Perhaps that's what led me to my dalliances in showbiz later in life. This fine elegant woman, too delicate in my eyes should not have left us.

Well what do you understand at such a juncture? Although I do remember wanting to keep one of her handbags! It was a nice scotch plaid one, very stylish and ladylike. I should have made sure I got it but it was never given to me - how camp would that have been? Then it was too early in life for the seeds of Edith Shagpile to have been sown, to be resurrected in my later act.

*****

Harold must have been driven by the practical need for me to have a replacement mother; for this eight-year old dependent to be nurtured, fed, watered, cared for and safe, to allow him to work like a dog for poor wages. There was no instant Department of Works and Pensions or Benefits Agencies then to pop into to make a claim for his circumstances. Manual work was his state benefit and the name of his game. It must also be remembered that this area, known loosely as the Black Country, took in part of the south Staffordshire coal mines and heavy industries and was one of the most polluted and disadvantaged areas of its time in terms of health in the country.

It was during the mid 1800s that the area began to become known as the 'Black Country'. There are many suspect origins as to how this name came to be used. Some say it is because of the bellowing of polluted furnaces and steel works together with the coalmining, which produced a black soot over the area; others claim it was due to the fact that the seams of coal were so near to the surface of the land that its appearance was that of very dark soil, which it would have been. The Black Country residents were, and still are, proudly fierce of their independence and, despite being in close proximity to Birmingham, see themselves as very separate from it. I heard someone say quite recently, "now I dow ever gooo there cock".

Learning to survive in those bleak, post-war days of that time (the war not being witnessed by me as I was born at the very end of 1949) it all seemed normal and worked! Yet then the social structures were different and unemployment was not a big issue as you could scrape out some work, providing you did not have too many aspirations beyond your place.

My new mother, my former cousin who I thought was an aunt, was named Edith Swann. She no doubt did her best but you can never feel the love and warmth of the one who I had believed was my birth mother. Any love I tried to feel or attachment to this often doom-laden, preoccupied, sad-looking and worried soul didn't seem to work. Her hard contribution to life had been to be a victim of circumstances, to rear her younger sister's children and again to allow her sister Fran the opportunity to work - no affordable paid nursery places then.

This marriage had happened and on top of that she was to look after her father, a veteran of the First World War and another remarkable survivor. She went to work in a factory called Walsall Conduits (perhaps the name of a double act?), then offices at times. She had left school with the main expectation to serve in the house and a life of demanding, quiet drudgery to look after others. You could see the disappointment of lost opportunity in her mournful eyes, together with often-expressed bitterness.

Because of these responsibilities we decanted to a small, solidly-built council house of hamster-like proportions, which was to be a sort of home for me for the next nine years. To resettle in our former house seemed not an option as Harold wanted to keep the peace. Having these, partly self-imposed, responsibilities must have been a turmoil and conflict for Edith. My haven there was a tiny box room at the front of this doll's house, but it could only be used at bedtimes, as that was its use. Not like today where a boy's room is an entertainment, electronics and computer centre for the modern child to escape in solitude to.

Edith's father, my former mother's older brother, was called Bob, Robert if you were posh. So we left behind the more spacious dwelling of Bolton Road on the other end of town. This, and many other similar properties, was owned by an uncle through another sister of Bob and Hannah called Rose. She was the wife of a man called Abraham and although he was not Jewish, he was somewhat of a pre- and post-war property mogul of his day, perhaps a bit like a Rachman of the times.

In the time before moving there my memories are of playing on an old tricycle I named Esmeralda! It was used to lug back shopping and carry errands and to play over Belchers Field, a wreck of a piece of bulbous, uneven land across the lane. Many an hour was spent on this tricycle, second-hand and painted black and cream. Well I could pretend it was a 1950s Armstrong Siddeley, a grand car for its day and, like me, a collectors piece for the discerning!

Also, walking with Hannah one dark evening, hand in hand as we walked back from some visit somewhere, there was a corner shop situated in our road called Johnson's with its blind down, yet clearly we could see a slap of tiles with a large barrel of cheese on display in the window. I stopped suddenly, jerking mother to a standstill to stare at this enormous cheese as, sat right in the middle of it, was a huge rat perched nibbling away on the top of it quite enjoying itself! Well I had never encountered a rat before and thought it quite nice! Mother pulled me away sharply saying, "We won't be going in there ever again!" What a pity poor little rodent.

In those days it wasn't the custom to sit in and watch the one or two channels on the tiny encased Bush TV sitting in the corner of the room. It was very much before any form of technology and computers, so I often went down a narrow lane at the side of some semi-grand houses, with the girl next door named Irene, which proved a good piece of entertainment.

*****

The infant and junior school I attended was named Holy Trinity and is still there. It was there that I had my first taste of dressing up when I was chosen to be a pageboy for the May queen. Dressed in satin and kept back in class with one of the mistresses undertaking her needlework, pinning and tailoring this fabric to my body. I learned to stay very still and dealt with the laughter of the other kids peering through the classroom windows at this spectacle of costume fitting. I was shy but loving it. It all seemed good fun - even prancing around the maypole and twirling in and out of a weaving mix of camp-coloured ribbons didn't seem to worry me, as countless of other of my generation seemed adept at it.

The house that I shared with Harold and Hannah seemed on reflection a happy place. I never understood it to be unusual not to have a separate bathroom and that twice a week a large tin bath would be filled with hot water in front of a roaring fire; not like the daily showering of our modern times today. However, the new house with Edith did have an upstairs bathroom. What luxury! A good wash-down in the previous dwelling was all that was required by a fastidious mother and her hot flannels and soft hands. I remember Hannah as gentle, calm and unthreatening. She showed love and gave cuddles. I recall once sitting in a chair whilst she was ironing when perhaps I wasn't getting too much attention. She looked over and told me how much she loved me. That I do remember with clarity, with a warm smile and a gentle tone. I was to come to miss this in abundance.

What seemed to be good times were not to last too long. In between bath days, it was all quite comforting as I recall. Tea (dinner to some) was always an occasion. It must have been good, wholesome grub, as there never seemed to be any left over. We sat around the table for all meals, no culture of isolation in a bedroom of computers or time alone without mother present. It all seemed good to me.

One abiding memory that sticks with me is that on Sundays in that house in Bolton Road, Harold always cooked. The image of him chopping sprouts so finely it could have been from a food processor of today's times, undertaken with such precision. Using a fork, he would beat them senseless then finely chop them with a knife so misshapen through years of abuse on the side of the saucepan it looked like an old Anglo-Saxon find. He continued this ritual up until his 80s!

*****

CHAPTER 2

Now returning to life with Edith, post Hannah. Once that marriage had taken place, I was now in residence in what felt like a foreign land, crammed in this small house where Edith had lived from pre-war years in Dial Lane. I look at it now as a place I would call 'Dial Lane for Murder', though I must say that in my recollection of it in those days it seemed neat, tidy and well maintained, but hardly a place of beauty today.

After her marriage, and being 39 or 40 years of age, she became pregnant, an unusual age of that day, and produced a sweet little bundle of light-haired fluff to be named Christine. I liked her and was very fond of holding her, buying her little presents and taking her out in her pram. I think I would have been 12 years old then but that novelty was to wear thin.

Edith was totally consumed and anxious towards Christine through her growing years. To my observations, even then as a youngster, it felt odd. She was dominated, controlled and idolised in equal measures, all at my expense. They call it sibling rivalry yet there was no rivalry on my part; I was generally tolerated and ignored. Poor Edith didn't know any better; she meant well no doubt. What effect all this obsessive input had on Christine I can only imagine. I certainly know it wasn't a good approach in which to foster a healthy development. I knew quite early on that I had to escape the incestuous life of the Black Country but could see, even then, how the fabric of this world hung together.

As the years flew by I don't think I was at my happiest, wanting in the recesses of my mind to escape that environment for good. It was claustrophobic, small-minded and even then, I felt that I didn't belong. My fantasy world took over, not entirely schizophrenic-like, but some coping mechanism must have kicked in as is often with kids. This is part of normal development. Many of my generation never desired to move away and I'll expand on this social dynamic at another juncture.

Somehow, I knew there was a better, more tolerant and exciting world out there. Edith had succeeded in alienating most of her remaining family. Even years before, the view of family life was of a world in a street together, poor but never truly lonely. This is still very much the case today in certain areas of the country including the Black Country. However, Edith's dear sweet sister, called Fran, who had her five kids growing up, rarely visited. Fran's husband, Ray, a good- natured man would occasionally pop in on his bike when riding past that way from his work. He never stayed long - no one did.

Once, I vividly recall being a very early teenager and Edith was pegging out her crisp washing in the garden. They had wooden props in those years that splintered and she was nagging and droning on at me when I cracked. Grabbing the prop, I wielded it like a medieval jouster, putting it an inch from her body and threatening to lance her head off if she didn't give me a break. And look at her mad behaviour as I pointed out in no meek way, she was defiantly more than one screw loose! I told her if she tried any retaliation I would most definitely, "get her". She threatened to tell, "yer dad". I told her to tell who the hell she liked - I was putting up with it no more, dad or not. Well it seemed it must have partly worked as there were no reprisals from, "yer dad" or it seemed so for a while from the mad woman herself.

*****

As I progressed to secondary school I was to make my two life-long friends, Vivienne and Gordon, who were eventually to marry in 1970, with me present and still very much in my life all these years later, with me still driving them mad! But more of them later...

The school was called Hill Top, now long-since demolished. It was a place of good solid education; quite harsh at times but disciplined and not always so foreboding. However, it did teach us to read and write, not so you would know that from this text! I loved history and art and generally avoided games by always managing to be allowed to miss classes to write plays and concerts for performances on the school stage, or even take part in a talent show. Wow, how progressive for the early 60s!

I loved English literature and language but never quite got the grasp of it as much as I would have liked. I loved at least being read to by Miss Jones, the only elderly female teacher in this then all boys' school, who had been brought in to pep up proceedings ready for amalgamation. With girls being kept at bay in the other half of the building we were all fascinated by what was going on over the other side of that fence, how apt that was to become in my life. Operating as two completely different institutions it was to remain segregated for around four years. I recall Miss Jones enthralling me with Nevil Shute and his, *'A Town Like Alice'*. Goodness, those bloody wartime Japs! The human spirit of survival is always amazing.

I used to call her Aunt Hettie. I have no idea why but I adored her; she was gentle, kind and tolerant even with unruly boys. The headmaster was named Mr Mansell and when the day came for amalgamation with the opposite sex, Miss Benfold, the headmistress of the girls' school, took charge. She was a huge big buxom lady and we named her The Wedge! She glided in at assembly to the sounds of Ken Cartwright, the music maestro, playing the *'Polonaise Symphony'* like a butched-up Liberace.

Jack Lowe was another good, tolerant teacher who never crushed my spirit and occasional mad antics. Maybe all this gave me some secret desire to entertain as I mocked the teachers, impersonated them and performed like a silly fool at any opportunity. There always is a class clown, isn't there? It's also a useful deterrent to have a few fellow students on your side when the bullies started.

I remember winning my first big applause in the big hall, impersonating Hilda Baker, copying some of her variety act with a chosen tall boy as the stooge to stand beside me. If you recall this great lady, she always had someone in silence gazing up to her, named Cynthia. The wonderful actress Jean Fergusson wrote and starred in the play of Hilda Baker's life in the 90s and it is some of the best theatre I have ever witnessed. She wrote the book, *'She Knows You Know!'*, the remarkable story of her life. This was published in 1997 and is not so easy to obtain but well worth trying to get. Thank you Jean, for my very personal copy from you.

The other big event that I recall was an interpretation of Max Wall as the mad professor, playing the piano and fooling around. I learned a few chords, spaced out my fingers and pretended with dramatic gestures that I could play classical music. Yes, I was a big con even then!

*****

It's amazing, but not so surprising that when Christine, my stepsister, did escape to a small terrace some ten-minutes' walk away, she was still in the clutches of the dominatrix (Edith) and it was almost as though she had not left home. I think she faced constant questioning and 'guidance' from her mother and, as a result, became more in turmoil than she should have been.

Her first marriage was doomed. Her husband was an inoffensive soul, not the brightest of buttons, but an escape avenue from this overbearing presence. Well that is what I believed he was. I am sure if I was to talk with Christine today she may not see it quite as I did in the distant haze of memory. Divorce came after producing one fine girl who looked amazingly like Christine (they do don't they?). This young girl was a fun little thing and often left in the care of the new grandmother, to its peril. Although by then even Edith may have learned from her mistakes and was never as harsh towards her as she had been with Christine. After meeting another guy, Christine cohabited with him to produce another lovely little boy who it turned out was to be reared by his father's mother and never to be close to his own.

Christine's daughter was very much granny-reared in order to allow Christine to work and provide. Tragically, this delightful, vulnerable teenager that she became, died after a hospital admission and a brief recovery period to be found breathless and gone in the bay window of her mother's home. This must have had tragic repercussions and emotive, complicated reactions as it affected the stepbrother very badly, who was very young at the time. Prior to this, she was in a relationship with someone else, which seemed to be built on fear and brutalisation, with the bullying that goes with it. No doubt, drink was involved in this type of character. I am sure she did confide in Edith but she stayed, as most battered soles do, for the intimidation and failure it produces in the victim, plus a very unhealthy dependency.

Those few times I met him, now older and a bit more experienced in summing up character, he was always kind and interested, and quite charming but without consistent work whilst Christine always did more than her share of employment. I never involved myself much and didn't know about all of this at the time. She had to make her own decisions and we all know how hard that can become when you may feel caught within unhealthy relationships. Once she did confide in me after the events, it was a time we may have been a little closer. However, I was well gone by now from these lives and only saw from afar those happenings. My training days had started, my flirtations with showbiz had begun and by 1969 I had fallen into a life with Dennis to create my own tapestry of life and future.

Returning, at least at the beginning, once a month to give Edith a few pounds to have her hair done, they acknowledged Dennis well and liked him. They took him to those strange hearts they had. "Good lad that Dennis", Harold would often state. Well that's quite something, I thought, coming from this inexpressive father. He could see the goodness in him for sure, and the steady hand he was wielding quietly in my life. What Edith ever did with that hair treat gift I'll never know. It surely never found its way to her head - she was more at home with a Twink perm! Goodness, the smell of those chemicals; it's amazing she never went bald!

Eventually, Christine was to escape her abusive relationship. God knows how but it meant alienation from her beautiful son who stayed with his father and his grandmother for his early experiences and formation. I don't know how he is getting along as I lost contact with him when he would be around 16. I wish him well.

Once again, Christine met another man, this one called Steve and they had one son together, called Steff and from that relationship she seemed to be more mature, settled and organised. It was in this time period that Christine tragically lost her only daughter from that first marriage that I have previously described. I last saw her at my Dennis's funeral in 2005 and briefly one time afterwards. You can see we are not an adopted family that is close.

Through the 80s and 90s she did attend some of my one-man shows, mainly at Cannon Hill Arts Centre in Edgbaston, but no permanent continuation of any relationship has been forthcoming. I hope she is happy and well, in particular those two sons - I hope they are dealing with life in a positive manner. I think they may have learned a lot. On balance, I see Christine as a good woman who did her best and she herself has not had life so easy and pain free, and has had to, in her own way, deal with difficulties as we all do.

CHAPTER 3

I didn't discover that I was adopted (big deal) till I was leaving secondary school. Thinking Harold and Hannah were my blood parents I was given a certificate, enclosed in a sealed envelope, by Edith to take to the school that I was due to leave the following year. Naturally, I opened it and it stood out clear even to a 15-year old that this was a certificate of adoption. Initially thinking that when Harold had married Edith that second time around they had adopted me for Edith's sake, I was to examine it further. I realised that I had originally been adopted by Harold and Hannah and, to date, not been told.

Sitting on this anxiety-provoking knowledge for almost two years, not knowing then how to approach this odd pair, as I saw them at that stage, I then asked the big question. I approached both Harold and Edith regarding my original adoption to see if I could at least find some facts regarding it. With Edith, I was met with pursed lips and defensiveness, and an embarrassed glint of sadness. She said, "Well you can ask your dad." He was sorting his veg in his immaculate garden with its one side dedicated to the home-grown variety. I calmly asked him if he could throw any light on the origins of the adoption, telling him that the only reason I needed to know was that the years are advancing and we need to deal with these things. Brave of me I think!

Well I am not too sure. He leaned on his spade, with no intention of striking me with it, and was calm. As he scratched his head he said, "Well your mother (Hannah) dealt with all that, it was a long time ago. I do know we fetched you from some big place near Wolverhampton, but as Hannah dealt with it all that's the only thing I can tell you."

"Oh big deal then." I thought. But also believing that such things undisguised in those days seeded the roots for future discontent. So at least I have that fact to blame on my personality malfunctions and any maladaptions - a useful scapegoat of blame when feeling self pity! Or when the chips are down! No, not me, I think, "Who Do You Think You Are?" A breakthrough, even to broach this, but no more information could I gather. I had told him I had all the original documents now as by the mid-70s the law on adoption information had changed, but the contents of these still left both me and him baffled. I was to relax my search for some years as I was too busy getting on with the here and now and only had so much time to dedicate to my own source of life. It could all wait.

As the years fled by, looking back, I did find the address where my birth mother had lived. It proved she had died some 12 months or so prior to the discovery and from talking to a neighbour of hers I was duly informed that she had 11 children in the area! My God, there is me thinking my early life was that of an only child and now to discover Mary (as she was named), had been a busy little soul!

I decided I didn't want to search any more and to live with any abandonment issues I have in this life as I had had so many. Besides, what if I did discover this new extended tree and what if I couldn't explain this story, as they may be as shocked as me to find out that, according to my new-found documents, the father is stated to be a Mr Thomas Care; not the father registered on the certificate of birth. No, best leave some things alone. I had come this far and it hadn't destroyed me yet, so why could or would this knowledge do so in the future? It's hardly life-threatening and may open many a can of worms and upset a few more lives, so why do it?

Edith lived on to 1997 and Harold struggled on quietly, with me making my visits more often on that awfully depressing drive. He used his survival instincts, deep in untold thoughts and carried on till I virtually forced him out of the hamster cage as his frailty became so evident. On he coped until 2005, the same period as Dennis's departure. Both seemed settled, comfortable, warm and fed as appetites would allow. By this time Harold was both depressive and delightful in equal measures; age had its mellowing effect. I took on the responsibility and practicalities for both he and Dennis, both now coming to their last stages. Our Victorian house in Flint Green Road, Acocks Green, was named Vernon Cottage; the Victorians often called them cottages despite their location in the suburbs of large towns. The house took on a homely nursing home atmosphere. I was Matron, obviously!

*****

In the last few years of Harold's life, he did shed more light on his own earlier exploits and experiences, something he could never have done in his younger age. The process of ageing really has some compensations at times. On probing and extracting from him more, he became more amenable to this tactic as I had the time to be careful how I did it. I discovered a little more about his wartime experiences. He was like many, an unsung hero of his generation. He told me he had been on 'manoeuvres' during the war somewhere off the coast for many weeks and they all knew something big was happening. Then one day the fleet took off and this was no exercise but what became known as the ill-fated Dieppe Raid.

He was one of the first generation of Royal Marines. I believe it was this battle, which earned them another coloured beret. He told me he had his wireless man with him - I got the impression these soldiers worked in little teams of around three as they disembarked from their flimsy amphibious craft. They disembarked to a tirade of machine gun fire and heavy artillery - they were being mowed down like blades of grass. They struggled to get to the beach. The Germans were just sitting waiting for them. They knew this prelude to the big D-Day was happening and were well prepared for them.

I was able to get a description from him that entailed him seeing his comrades' bodies floating and sinking into the water as he also went beneath the waves for some impossible protection. He said, "They didn't stand a chance." A bullet ripped into his own upper arm followed by another. He believed his time was up, but on resurfacing the shellfire had abated and the Germans lined up the survivors and marched them into the town. By some fate, he had survived this military disaster.

He recalled being patched up in some field hospital, then was eventually transported to a POW camp. I was totally amazed that I was extracting so much thoughtful recall at all. It was quite moving. He described being there, "It was very basic," he said, "I just got on with it." Yet Red Cross parcels did arrive at times - almost like a child having a small treat. He was transported to a work camp in Poland and his time was spent in working groups felling large trees in the forest under German watch. He described one German guard as being friendly and sharing cigarettes. His name was Hans. He then launched into explaining the correct way to fell a tree, describing it as a useful experience!

As a child on my single bed, I had an extraordinary crocheted blanket. Harold had learned the craft and brought it back to England, eventually to find its way onto my bed to warm my body. I couldn't even cast on! Also, as a young child I asked him about his unusually formed muscular upper arm with its funny scars and what they were but he was never forthcoming.

He recollected that due to the war not now going in the Germans' favour he was guarded less, as rumours prevailed that the allied forces were on the offensive and getting nearer to the camp. It was at this opportunity that he made his escape with a fellow prisoner and absconded without too much of a problem as, by now, the Germans were more interested in their own preservation and were somewhat lax on their charges. His flight out of Poland now took place, as this was where he had been transported to work out his war.

Also known as Operation Rutter, the Dieppe Raid that was responsible for my father's incarceration was intended to seize and hold, for a short while, a major port. This was both to prove it was possible and also to gather intelligence from captured prisoners as well as an opportunity to destroy coastal defences. None of the major objectives was achieved and a total of 3,623 of the 6,086 who made it ashore were either killed, wounded or captured.

The force was made up of the brave Canadian troops consisting of around 5,000 and 1,000 British of which 275 commandos (one whom was my father) were killed wounded or captured. Royal Navy losses were very significant, losing one destroyer, 33 landing craft with another 550 dead or wounded. The Royal Air Force fared no better with the loss of 100 aircraft and nearly 100 casualties or prisoners. The German forces, on the other hand, lost fewer than 50 aircraft and 590 of their ground forces were killed or wounded. Placing this against the numbers game of winners and losers in such a war theatre, in military terms the repelling of the raid proved an overwhelming success for the Germans.

Harold was less able to give exact details of his adventurous return but did describe being put up, at some risk, by a Polish farmer and his wife in a barn and that it was the very first time he had experienced a feathered down-type duvet which he raved about. In view of his reluctance throughout his life to tell or recall anything, I was more grateful than he will ever know for this insight. He must have somehow got to Italy as he also described that 'traitors' (could it have been Mussolini?) were hung upside down in the town square. This, in terms of timescale, did not seem clear but I did not press him on this as I was happy to get anything out of this old soldier.

Looking back at the historical information regarding this Dieppe Raid it is remarkable to think that the allied reconnaissance was unable to detect the heavy defences dug in on the cliff tops around the area and shows how clever the Germans had been at hiding their strength of position. They were able to fool any aerial photographs to detect them. It has often been believed, due to the fact the Germans were on high alert, that some tip-off was not so unexpectedly picked up through radio transmissions and monitoring of the increased English coastal activity.

After months of running loose on the continent Harold somehow got a ship with others back to the shores of England; he had made it home at last. He described how he was demobbed (he still had his demob suit in his bedroom wardrobe which he wore at his daughter's wedding years later and it still fitted!). He was given around a two-pound pension on his discharge. However, as he returned eventually to work, he lost that entitlement and never bothered to pursue it further.

I also learned that as a very young man he was living with five brothers in a back-to-back tenement and that one night his mother went up to bed with a lighted candle which fell into her nightwear and she suffered a high degree of burns. She lived on in hospital for a few weeks before succumbing to eventual death.

Harold, once I got him loosened up in old age, described how he visited her each day but never saw her as she was swathed completely in bandaging from head to toe. The sigh of pity and brokenness was evident on his face, as I don't believe he had ever told a living soul before. He said, "She never had a chance. She was like an Egyptian mummy lying there." Life was tough for this generation more than we will ever know or imagine.

My opinion of him changed from being a cold, heartless man to one I was beginning to understand, who had coped, like Dennis, sealed off from his torment. How can we ever know these things unless we dig them out sensitively like old roots? The human spirit and coping ability is remarkable. Another factor that I discovered was his amazing ability of using HB pencils to sketch. Hidden in a draw I found some amazing delicate portrait pictures of great skill. When asked about them he amazingly confessed, "Oh yes, I passed to go to art school but we couldn't afford that so I didn't bother."

*****

Another abiding memory I recall was after Hannah had died and over the intervening weeks and months before Harold's eventual re-marriage. If I was away from school at holiday times or there was no one around to keep an eye on me, especially if he had to work a weekend, I was picked up by him in this huge old lorry (strangely enough named a Dennis) and taken to the factory where he was working. I was dropped off at the caretakers' little house in the grounds.

I remember they were called Mr and Mrs Tolliday. They were very warm-hearted and kind to me and dad seemed to have made a good friend of them, as Mr Tolliday also worked doing other jobs there too. Once, I was taken onto the factory floor and I had never seen working conditions like it. Remember I was only eight or nine then. Even I could see the heat of these furnaces and the black faces of young and old men doing these hard manual jobs, beating steel, pushing metal into flaming, cavernous, heated ovens. I couldn't even begin to wonder how they stood it but they did, these men were tough, no nonsense; what else could they be? They were friendly and there was obviously great camaraderie. It must have been just like the war. I definitely knew even then that I could and never would be part of that slave labour; I was just transfixed and looked on in awe.

Royal Marine, artist and unsung hero. From an anonymous man Harold grew in stature in every way to me, as he needed me more and more. Even saying at one point in a quiet voice, looking me direct in the eyes, "I am ever so glad we had you." This unemotional, matter of fact man who displayed so little was so revealing in his vulnerability. Who knows the real man he was or could have been if circumstances and his life had been different? We grow reflective in old age but do we speak it out? Is there anyone there to take note or to even care?

When my GP, a lovely man, came to visit this sick ward at Vernon Cottage I was quite manic, greeting him at the door saying, "Do you want gerontology, oncology or the psychiatric crash bed?" The latter was for me as I dashed from one room to the other, attending to the needs of these two souls, both quietly knowing their fate. I would, despite his frailty, manage to get 'dad' up the stairs which took some navigational skills as they were steep and abundant, in a slow, careful, time-consuming manner, always asking him to say goodnight to Dennis in the middle room before he embarked on his upward spiral. He wasn't always keen to do so but I always opened the door for them to see each other so they could engage a little. Harold would look wistfully and say to Dennis, "What a pair of old codgers we are Dennis. What a state to be in and this poor lad having to do all this."

Taking him to the loo and settling him in took a good half hour but he was comfy and ready to sleep and seemed at peace for this short while, ready for his bath the next day. Putting him in his bath to supervise his basic needs, of which he had no compulsion in letting me do, he realised for his own dignity he had to let me. This intensely private man went from the most insular person I had known to allowing me to nurse him in the most intimate way any one could.

I knew that if ever Harold was to be admitted to hospital it would be the end of him, so I resisted this. After some tests and blood were taken my GP said he would need to be admitted in order to monitor and check on a daily basis levels that may be affecting his thyroid. I knew that, under secretions, he would be left lethargic and in a low state and it must be treated; this could not be undertaken at home. I had no choice but to let him go as this monitoring arrangement could not be maintained at home.

I was not a happy Bunny, as I knew he wouldn't get the individual attention I could give him. I was right. Even on his admission, I started the discharge process by seeing his attached social worker to get a plan ready and make a future for him by planning some adaptations and aids to Vernon Cottage, the Acocks Green house. I promised him I would get him back home to me as soon as all his levels were stabilised. I knew the nursing care was going to be poor, I could smell it. He wasn't nursed in any consistent way. He was packed into an overcrowded ward with a lack of staff continuity. Meals and medications were not ensured or given and monitored, being left alone, and lockers were out of reach. The usual poor, to no, attention to detail at all.

I did early morning swoops to check on him. I told staff the best position to nurse him in - they must have loved me! "Upright for his condition." It all fell on deaf ears. What chance do you have if there is no one to advocate for you? However, whilst still at home, Dennis and he were at least afforded more dignity and attention, which they deserved.

After attending to Harold when still at home, I would then return to the 'lower ward' in the house to see to my dearest dependant Dennis. I was no martyr. It was a case of getting on with it, as I had not had to do so much in the past for the two of them. Now they really needed it; now was payback time. It's interesting to me that when I was clearing out the old house, which Harold had spent almost 40 years in, the only things I had kept were the old 1960s Dansette record player and many old photographs. The record player from that era is an iconic image, I suppose. It now sits in my attic in my home in Mid Wales.

Amazingly, both Dennis and Harold died within a few days of each other and, as we all know who experience such things, life goes on somehow. But how? As for these writings, who knows where they will spill next?

*****

CHAPTER 4

Moving on now from the bleakness of the 50s came those heady 60s, which for many of that generation, on reflection, was dynamic and socially revolutionary. Really! Two years' of jobs lie ahead. At one point I became a soils laboratory tester. I hadn't a clue what I was doing and left before they found me out. Then a furniture shop assistant, basically humping settees and chairs from huge vans and shoving them in storerooms.

One job I did take to as a 16-year old was in a gentlemen's outfitters. I just got off a bus one day and walked into Jones and Co., in the High Street, West Bromwich. It was like something from a 1930s movie with the amazing characters of Mrs and Miss Jones, mother and daughter, who had been in the business for what seemed like centuries and the shop looked like it had too - it was incredible. What I could do with an inside leg, a pair of combinations and a Viyella shirt was no one's business, and what could be arranged on a headless bust could be quite adventurous. These odd, eccentric, real ladies, were a great influence on my life.

Just imagine Hinge and Bracket, if you are old enough to recall. They were the personification of that type, but real. The fun and laughter we had in that blast from the past was unimaginable. There were just two of us, myself and a guy called Alan whom I had known from my old school and was trusted as a sort of manager. We used to dress and change the window each week, crawling into the space on our bellies to replace glass shelves held up on dainty supports; one slip and it could all come crashing down. This window burst with shirts, kipper ties, cufflinks, starched collars, and an array of designer jumpers, all stuff that could now grace an antique fair.

We played up blind. We would impersonate the ladies whilst doing this whole-day task. One afternoon, Tessa, the daughter, strode into the shop, asked us if we would like tea and calmly stated with a wry smile, "Of course we can hear everything you say in the window boys." Little did we realise the two vents in the window at the top acted as a sound system direct in to the ladies' lounge above!

The other juvenile thing I would do each Monday morning, after seeing Diana Rigg in *'The Avengers'* on the black and white TV (to think I would meet her a little later), was to charge into the shop taking on her role in an assault mode and proceed to attack the all-in-one bust. Standing erect on its pedestal with either a dressing gown or shirt and tie immaculately displayed on it, grabbing it I would chop at it, throw it around the shop, throw it over my back and leave it even more lifeless on the floor. After these antics, I would then have to spend half an hour repairing and hiding the damage I may have done, so that the Joneses couldn't detect it. One morning, Tessa came hurriedly into the shop, eyes direct, and said wistfully, "I see you have been watching *'The Avengers'* again." She then swept back through her door like a fairy godmother who knew all, but tolerated these antics from these young lads.

I had been like many a staunch *'Avengers'* fan, eventually pulling off a coup, managing to get supporting artist's work through knowing and meeting, by then, a repertory of actors at the Alexandra Theatre in Birmingham. *'The Avengers'* was filmed at the Elstree Studios, Boreham Wood where I wheedled my way into production at what was then Associated British Pictures. Meeting my idols Patrick Macnee, Diana Rigg and appearing guest star Peter Wyngarde. I was to meet up with him again some eight years later. He is an intriguing and enigmatic man, who I will return to later in these pages.

It was well after this and I had started my training when I remember going to an exhibition at the now long-disappeared Bingley Hall, the main centre for things like the forerunner to the Ideal Homes events and the like. It was also a large entertainment venue and I went along to see some old performers, basically from the music hall generation who may still be remembered by some of you older readers.

Tessie O'Shea and Sandy Powell were two opposite performers who made quite an impression at a time when they would be considered out of step with the late swinging 60s and they were great. Family favourites with generations before me.

Tessie was sometimes known as 'Two Tonne Tess'. She was a big girl and was a true pro with a big smile, singing brisk songs clutching her banjolele, ending her act with a burst of quick finger magic on this instrument with all the pluck she could give it. A big stage personality - that crowd loved her.

Sandy Powell, whose famous catch phrase was, "Can you hear me mother?" delighted the crowd with his act as a pretty appalling ventriloquist with the dummy falling apart as his routine went on. On this occasion, he seemed to be dressed as what resembled a Chelsea pensioner. To see this old pro performing was a lesson in survival from one era into another. Sometimes assisted by his wife, who would pop on to help him, it was great amusing fun to have witnessed these two performers.

*****

I wandered into psychiatric nursing in 1968, a year before I met Dennis.

In 1968, for some reason, I undertook some voluntary days at the then named Hallam Hospital in West Bromwich, now known as the local district general hospital. It was here that I met a post-graduate student, who launched at me enthusiastically to say, "You would be very good at psychiatric nursing." She was qualified in the mental handicap field; I knew nothing of the differences nor what I was letting myself in for.

She gave me a list of hospitals, writing them down for me, and encouraged me to write to them, which I duly did. These places, I discovered, were either for people with degrees of mental handicaps together with some physical impairment or for individuals with varying problems relating to mental illness. At that stage of life, I knew very little, if anything, of such importance and difference.

In those days of the mid- to late-60s these institutions were referred to as Subnormality Hospitals and the others were Mental Hospitals. Usage of words and socio-political trends and correctness tend to change approximately every five years but have the same meanings. It's all to do with the way we use them and tag them, or not, to individuals with these complex problems.

I wrote off some letters, as said not knowing the distinct differences between each of those specialities. One response arrived from the Chief Male Nurse of Highcroft Hospital, based in Erdington, Birmingham. I also received three further invites from others I had written to. However, for no reason I could think of, I decided to attend that first response and present myself at the gates and imposing doors of Highcroft Hospital. (Amazingly, I was to return to Highcroft Social Club in 1990 and do my act there. It was crowded and a great night certainly for me and by the reaction of that crowd, for them to.)

Being 18 years old, slim, eager and smartly dressed, cutting a youthful dash, I entered the grand office of Mr McFarland to be interviewed there and then. After around 15 minutes, I was told to go to the nurse training school (to be called one day The Nurse Education Centre). The phone call had been made by McFarland in my presence to Mr George Ivory, The Principal Tutor, "as I must become a student and join the next intake", where I was to be 'trained' according to the syllabus laid down by the G.N.C. To think one day I would be a senior tutor, entertainer and part time poof!

*****

Having taken the obligatory entrance exam and made the sufficient score, I was duly accepted to attend the next of the students' intake. Yet before that I was obliged to work as an assistant to gain insight and practical experience as a testing ground to see if I would hack it. The camp green epaulettes helped by a nice little top and starched white coat was my uniform. It was a nice touch yet was I never to get my hands on a floppy starched matron's hat! Well you can't have everything in life, can you? (Although I often wore one behind screens, in cupboards and any place I could get away with it to lighten the daily load.) I later used to sneak one home and wear it to surprise Dennis, the poor sod!

Six months of probationary period really had my eyes opened and stuck them open for the rest of my life. I was placed on a third floor ward named St. Barnabas, which housed 44 elderly gentlemen. Some of these patients, well most of them, were confined to a place resembling a near perfect-looking medical ward. The routine was relentless and unforgiving but my, how those days sped by. No one was left dirty, unattended or unobserved, as it was more than your own life was worth. Should there be special treatments, and there were many, they would be undertaken in order and precision. For a short while, I thought I had entered a general hospital but it doesn't take too long to spot the difference.

This far from saintly ward was shiningly clean. Its immediate impression was one of order but with a reasonable degree of permissiveness. Not only was I to learn about differing mental illness in the elderly and degrees of incapacity and memory loss, but also the sterile, non-touch techniques of the steriliser and then the replacement system of the packs of sterile supplies that succeeded them. Laying up trays and trolleys one minute, getting someone into the bath the next, you were accompanying a clinical procedure, undertaking the dressing of wounds, taking temperatures, respirations and the pulse. It was also here that I was shown how to take blood pressures properly. Occasionally an experienced person came, showed and explained what was going on and how to do it. You were soon left alone but checked up on - all was good enough once deemed competent. The giving of injections was an expectation upon you as early as your first year of training - that upper outer quadrant of the buttock will stay with me and my syringe forever.

I did meet kindness, gentleness and harshness in equal measures. If you were sharp, observant and spotted the dynamics and how it all stuck together, it is what one called a steep learning curve. Each varying environment was to have its own style, ethos, principles and groups. If you could remain open-minded to some extent, mouth partly buttoned, till you knew you had a voice that would be listened to, you could work wonders.

Witnessing the different souls admitted here in deteriorated mental and physical conditions and decline will always be with me and even in what seemed to be some of those darker days, some improvements and discharges were still effected. Relatives of some did visit and I realised there was a community out there that people not only came from, but even returned to.

It was a good consolidating experience, which helped for when I commenced the more formal element of this training and educational experience. It was all to help in understanding both the theories and the practice of dealing with such things, such as a failing memory, its causations and responses. It was also the beginning of my understanding of the personality in its various complex behaviours. To start to get an appreciation of the seriousness of schizophrenia, mood or affective disorders and the less serious, but equally incapacitating, neuroses of which we all experience to some degree. Studying the effects of institutionalisation was of particular interest and was to set me up to challenge and dissipate it as much as possible through my forthcoming stop-start career. You can never destroy it, even in a community, but you can minimise any potential effects. Like all times, things were beginning to change but at a more rapid pace. Psychiatry generally was opening up, more dynamic and many mixed-models of care were evolving and quickly if you wanted to pioneer them and have a go. It became somewhat of a passion for me.

*****

The admission wards were another world apart, all of them with a different culture of their own, depending who was running them. On one, B1, every patient admitted was asked to, or told to, take all their clothes off to be put into a large personal box which was then locked safely away. The idea was that they would initially be in bed for 24 hours to see the doctors and to be assessed in order to determine treatment options. Some were up and about quickly whilst others who were seriously, perhaps endogenously depressed, were to stay there to receive intro-muscular therapy of amitriptyline for the first few days under strict observation, then to commence after some days an oral suspension of the same medication. Some of these patients told us after that they felt they were in hospital and that something definite was happening to them, especially once they had improved and been discharged. Others must have found it frightening and horrific. This was a drug of choice, especially with older people with deep depressive states, and was first started in 1961, to be superseded now by a whole new generation of what are SSRI medications, which are generally much safer and far less toxic and unpleasant.

ECT (Electroconvulsive therapy) was also common in its use. A therapy first formulated in the late 1930s, now somewhat modified and given with a muscle relaxant and a drug to dry up bodily secretions. From this point of view, it was safer than its previous usage. Many people who were not around to see these things are now horrified by its use, but I was and still am open-minded about it, particularly when all else has failed over long periods of suffering, providing it is highly selected and agreed upon by all concerned. Never being a first line option. Theories were just as fascinating, but most of that for me came later, putting it into practice was what it was all about then.

One part of the training was to be placed with the district nurses, mainly all female at that time on my placement. As we gathered to be allocated our respective companion nurse for the day, mine was not so keen, I felt, to have this young male student. As we left the clinic from where to go on our patients' visit, the others walked into the car park and trundled into cars with what seemed a friendlier bunch of district nurses, to take them on their way. This I couldn't believe. I was walked to a black bicycle with a basket on the front, given an address about two, maybe more, miles away and told to meet this sour-faced pudding there. Well dears, I felt such a fool, so I imagined I was Beryl Reid in *'The Killing of Sister George'* and peddled for my life to wherever it was I was meant to be. I think the old misery was surprised to see me arrive, thinking I may fly off back to where I had come from, "No", I thought, "Madam, you won't beat me."

These experiences do one of two things come the future and you are in a position of influence. You either remain bitter and treat others the same, or you make sure you do not repeat these people's cruel ways and make sure they get the best quality experience you can involve them in. I had many ward experiences like that, remote people whose contact with both patient and student was controlled, so less was made of what could have been achieved. I hope I was never to follow that path, besides it's laughable now. To think I witnessed in 1968, on a non-training ward, patients queuing in a line, half dressed, waiting their turn in an open bathroom to be douched and cleaned and the water being changed only after three individuals had been completed. Then it would have helped to have had more than two working bathrooms between 76 people! And to think back then the hospital provided the most inappropriate clothes – suits, trousers, thick shirts and ties and most wore a collar and tie in all weathers. Thank goodness that wasn't common practice for long, but was an imbedded part of institutional life from the earlier generations.

It wasn't unusual to be phoned by an assistant matron from the other side to go over to a disturbance on the female wards, as now there was a new era of co-operation emerging. Off we would fly to any ward to help quell a disturbance with as little but effective force these male nurses could provide, when it all got a little out of hand for our female colleagues. I think initially they must have thought that's all we did. It was not an uncommon sight to be restraining some huge, bellowing, screaming person, deluded and lashing out with all their weight and flaying arms to full effect. This was well before any formal training in the art of break away and control and restraint trainings grew into an industry some years in the future. I was to discover some of these female versions of nurses were quite good. I was impressed!

You would always know if a busy night had been had on other wards if you came on duty early in the mornings in those days. The smell of paraldehyde was toxic in the air. This drug was first known about and used in varying forms from 1882. It was even used in industry in forms. It induces rapid sleep in certain doses and has very little therapeutic use other than that it is highly effective. As 30 per cent of it is excreted by the lungs it gives off a very strong, unpleasant smell on the breath and to all around. It is colourless and does not react at all well with plastics, hence glass and glass syringes and metal needles had to be used; drawing up, placed into the kidney dish, covered with a dressing cloth, then on your way to deliver it, often in the backside. Some mornings the air was thick with the stuff. I swear I can still smell it now. Of course, this gave way a long time ago to less vile solutions but interestingly, even now it is used by some, particularly when status epilepticus occurs as it does not depress vital centres as much as the current drugs used today. Status epilepticus is where the person falls into deep, continuous, epileptic, uninterrupted fits.

Later on, becoming a tutor and senior tutor, these experiences made me understand how people should be managed. Loads of students passed through our fingers and many faces come to me now, even if their names have faded at all those places I went. I wish to think I made a difference and encouraged them to challenge the status quo; how to plan and really work out the dos and don'ts of care, giving intelligent descriptive incidents and patients to manage and deal with in the most informed way possible, and producing case studies in practice of how you manage the care from admission to discharge. Practising and honing their interactions, responses and interpersonal skills was the biggest part of what I believed training should be all about. If any of you may ever read this, let me know if I failed or succeeded! Many of these once great students went on to do good things by staying clinically involved and practising their best as others have fled up that pole to other dizzy heights and I wish them all well. I wonder where Colin Smith is today?

*****

In those days we were not attached to universities. We had not given up our independence of training and the education of staff was provided by schools of nursing, then colleges of nursing, which provided a feeling of belonging to a specific school and, with it, some sense of pride. It became the educationalist agenda by the 1980s to achieve academic status and give up the previous scheme of an apprentice-style system for a recognised academic one. This became fraught with problems and developed a separatist elite in some minds that has not quite mended with the passage of time. It's fair to say this could in hindsight have been managed better but it was the current political and social agenda that drove this through so that, in effect, those old colleges of nursing became absorbed into faculties of health. A different breed of student evolved from this university system that sprang from the old established polytechnic system.

I think my generation of practitioners did make a difference as much as social change was happening and impacting on lots of services. Later, I was to become an examiner and contribute to the setting of the state final examinations. Setting relevant questions to tax the mind beyond the obvious and draw the best consideration out of the students. There were practical and continued assessments also. Yet that final examination was all-important. Now it's mainly continuous assessment upheld internally and modified by panels and allied to academics and clinicians and is more complex than a road-map to peace. Examinations at stages of training with some external relevant body to nursing like the NMC should, or could, reintroduce a more focused exam system. I could uphold that but in my mind, and from what I observe, it appears to be virtually vanished. What goes around comes around - beware. I can hear them now, "Oh hark at him! Maudling for the old days." Sod them all!

We need knowledgeable doers. Then some of the evolutionary mess could get tidied up in a modern health care system. There are still great nurses out there, still as dedicated as ever. Ok, some have green hair and piercings - perhaps they are the new variety performers too. There are, of course, upsides to the new generation of nurses. In fairness, they are more adept to being mini-doctors and don't need to spend hours undertaking what may appear mundane tasks that in my days in training were sometimes spent. They undertake, in general nursing at least, more clinically-sophisticated procedures and more invasive techniques. They should be more evidence-based in their practice and the other argument would be why do I need a university degree to do tasks that are not essential and can be done by well-trained care workers? It depends on that individual as to how much they decide to input other things or lead from the front.

Today, it's an indictment of a once-proud profession that was based and trained at the coal face, when 'guidance' has to be sent to all registered nurses to tell them they must hydrate patients, feed them and ensure medications are taken and not left on lockers and bedsides, out of reach. Like the drinking water often is. Assistance is actually required to be given by the nurse - that means handing them the drink! And staying to ensure they take it. These simple, obvious things are just not always done. What the hell is nursing supposed to be about? That means the registered nurse as well as the burdened care worker. Even for the great registered nurse, please set by example and move from your tick boxes and computers and nursing stations, fight your way out of your present predicament. You may see human suffering in your own loved ones and be prompted to engage yourselves.

What has happened is that nurses no longer identify with a group of proud individuals in a college of pride, but a university of political and social upheaval and sometimes indifference that has no true vested interest in the practical care of a human beings to prevent them developing bedsores and the like. It has started to become a theoretical concept, out-balanced in practice, strangled by regulation and inter-professional rivalries.

There is no problem in obtaining academic status but not at the expense of hands-on practical care - we must never be too grand to do it. Nursing is led by the only group of people who should know how to give it, the registered nurses, so get back to it even if only occasionally to motivate sometimes flagging staff. There have been some returns to what I mention but it's going to take another big shift. In truth, ward leadership, commitment and motivation by those who can really make a difference.

Perhaps someone may have the idea of providing schools of nursing once more, where those academic links can still be kept. But not at the expense of people being trained thoroughly to benefit those in our charge. All is about rights but don't forget responsibility. Ok, I'll shut my gob now

Lacking in such things as hoists, lifts and apparatus, ergonomic assessments were a concept of the future. You needed to be resourceful and energetic, fit of sorts. Being young and healthy helped. At just turned 18, I was still very slim and with the energy you got with youth in those days. As for health and safety, I didn't know the concept - raised much above what used to be called common sense. Those small essential things of sitting people in a good position, cleaning out and refreshing an encrusted and foul-tasting mouth were all part of the day. Besides, I thought I was Hattie Jacques!

No wonder the glamour of showbiz loomed in my head. How could I ever do pantomime here? Yet it was one big production itself. Whatever happened to *'Goldie Locks and the Three Bears'*? Entertainment became an antidote to the systems and misery you could be engulfing yourself in - it could keep me fresh and sane, I thought.

*****

One thing I always said to my students was that I remember a tutor once telling us we should not get involved with our patients - this is rubbish. In order to be a good psychiatric practitioner you have to be involved with them. The skill and the art is in knowing how to handle that involvement, it's that which will set you apart from the mediocre.

Very early on in 1968, I was to work on a ward of 76 survivors of the First World War. Old and decayed, some of them were the remnants of a worldwide pandemic of flu that left its wake of disorder and brain diseases. This ward was spread over three floors. Soon, a few years later it was to become six smaller units. I realised how stupid it all was, having to carry the more physically-challenged from a top floor to the ground at meal times! No lift was available at that juncture. Some came down earlier to become bored, uninspired and complacent. Some were noisy and agitated. Were they upstairs because they made the place look untidy perhaps?

It was in these early days that I met Paul Beard, a brilliant nurse and a third-year student at the time, who was to become a lifelong friend, yet still going our eventual separate ways. To think he went to stage school to tap and dance and thought he may become the next Margot Fonteyn! A dynamic, difficult but loving personality he was rewarded with the OBE from Queen Elizabeth a few years ago for his services to the bewildered. He was also to stay around as a lifelong friend. Dennis also was fond of this energised character and would have been proud to see Paul recognised had he lived to have seen it.

Now I must introduce a character whom I will call Robert. After a brief spell in the nurses' home (male, of course) Robert and I shared a flat together, if you could call it that. We were so poor Robert, as I called him, not Bob, would often count out the potatoes to ration them for the week. We took on another lodger to help pay the bills in this freezing hellhole and a landlord who was struggling downstairs with a paranoid schizophrenic wife who would bang on the walls, telling the voices to go to hell. Not only that but she would scream at her visual and auditory hallucinations to such an extent the ambulance would arrive after a week or so of this and take her to All Saints Hospital. We were at Highcroft Hospital, so we had no conflict of interest did we! Talk about coals to Newcastle. Throughout this period, I referred to my friend Robert as 'Matron'.

I had gone to share this flat as by this time Robert had been involved with his first male partner after years of convincing himself he was a straight guy. Really! The way she swished! It was at this time I invented a new therapy called 'Slap Therapy'. By this time I had met a few actors from the repertory theatre in Birmingham as a distraction from the chores of nursing and knew how to slap without giving too much pain. I brought this into being after his lover, a big black handsome, charming brute who was a qualified nurse and deputy charge at the hospital, decided to uproot and go to live and work in North America. Robert was beside himself, it was an agonising time for him (come to think of it, his whole life has been agonising both for himself and for others). On the evening of his departure, with Robert waving him off at Liverpool, if I remember correctly, he returned and for a few nights was sobbing uncontrollably. Quite understandably.

I decided I had had enough and with all the therapeutic skill and sensitivity I could muster, along with acceptance and tolerance, I pulled him up from the sofa, shook him vigorously and bawled at him, "He's left you, silly! Get a f*****g grip!" I slapped him, shook him a little more and threw him back on his chair. How's that for psychiatric skill? I then made us a nice cup of tea! It worked - he took a reality check and I think it may have been the start of a new beginning. He has been spoiled ever since.

We went on to find a larger apartment - how posh - and there was to be five of us sharing that. It was a large Victorian double-fronted property in the 'fashionable' suburb of Lozells. This faded, grand old house was a perfect fit for our delusional minds with a non-working phone in the hallway, an intercom that did not connect and a large chandelier in one room. Even faded, royal blue, velvet curtains graced the large bay window. Heaven! Some of the goings on there would have been comparable with a Brian Rix farce.

We now had John to come live with us, the son of an army captain and a charming mother who stood firmly by their son. John would eventually become Jane, the best female conversion on this planet, a beautiful person with an equally amazing life and we are close friends today. What memories we shared and still do. She runs her own successful business and is a delight to be with. What that woman can do with her musical instruments has to be seen to be believed. An ardent animal rights campaigner, at one time the secretary of a cat protection league. She knows how to care for a pussy! She is talented and has an unusually good set of friends but is always so busy working still, as her skills are so much in demand.

It was always a delightful experience going to all her previous flats and houses as her tales and visitors were a constant source of drama and amusement, as she herself has a great humorous personality. We once dressed in drag together in late 1968 and she had an ageing Austin A40.

This seemed to bounce like a circus car - I never saw anyone drive with her legs crossed before!

She wanted to test out if I could get away with the dragging lark. I was terrified but entered into the spirit of it. This was well before her conversion and removal of the three-piece suite. Firstly, she pulled into the petrol station. In those days an attendant came and filled you up! "Hello girls! Going anywhere nice?" We smiled, responded quietly and, with a retiring air of class, paid the man who gave us an even bigger warm smile. Jane then decided to queue up at a well-known burger van in Colmore Row in Birmingham where we took our turn with a few wolf whistles. We of course ignored them, my heart was pounding - I was getting away with it! We must have been there ten minutes, yet it seemed an eternity. The thrill of this; my first major acting role. Jane was a natural and has always been so, but me? No wonder, some six years later I got my Equity Card!

The times that Jane was working from our flat she would be doing the make up and hair of some of the 'street girls' who she befriended and in the next room would be sitting a police woman who we knew well with her panda car prominently parked outside. What a giggle that was! Amazingly, years later the aforementioned policewoman crashed her own panda car right into other stationary police vehicles - she was as pissed as a newt! Goodbye to another promising career.

*****

CHAPTER 5

There is a large venue in Birmingham known as the Nightingale Club. It first started life as a place that gay folk could go and it became very popular. It was founded by two important people, Laurie Williams who was its secretary and manager, and a grandly-spoken gentleman named Derek Pemberton, who was its first chairman.

It was 1969 when its doors first opened - I say doors as it was on the site of an old ramshackle, former Indian restaurant. It became so well used they introduced membership and I was one of the first to be a member. The building consisted of what was a two up and two down, with the down section knocked partly through to make a small café with a few stools to eat your snacks from. There was a kitchen area that could muster up a snack, often served up by Ray who ran that for years. Tamla Motown was always blasting out with all those other hits of the day - you could even have a slow romantic dance around and look at the shimmering eyes of your partner! To think this was the year of the infamous Stonewall riots of New York. There was still a lot of campaigning in front of the more motivated community to make much difference regarding equalisation in many aspects of the law. This was partly forced upon the country, being a more European-wide resolution that had been adopted by more progressive attitudes abroad, despite what British politicians may have us believe.

The Nightingale soon outgrew its capacity and by 1975, and becoming a membership co-operative, moved to more suitable premises though a little further out, but still a manageable distance to Witton Lane near Aston and a stone's throw from the Aston Villa football ground. Many characters graced these places and cabaret was also being demanded and enjoyed. So, from 1975 until 1981, it ruled supreme as the premier gay venue in the city. My friend, Alan Leighton, broadcaster, journalist and TV personality, together with myself officially opened this venue. It was here I think I first saw and met Mark Fleming who I will talk at length about in these pages.

1981 saw the club move to its most central location to date, a superb site in Thorpe Street near the side of the Birmingham theatre, the

Hippodrome. Here it was to build growing success and deal with challenges right up to 1994. I was never a totally gay performer doing only gay venues, though on occasions I have done them including, in the past, two of the older Nightingales.

My friend Malcolm Baldwin, naming himself 'Melody Baldwin, Barmaid to the Stars' was its general manager during some of this time. I was able to get Joan Turner booked there and also the legendary Kathy Kirby came shortly before she quit showbiz. I hope it was nothing to do with us!

Malcolm was a funny man with loads of talent and an eye for what was good, having been head of entertainment on cruise ships - how apt he was here cruising his stuff. We became close friends at that time. He was also to design many a costume for me. He invented a character named Zena Lavoroni who was Malcolm's fictitious daughter who could do everything that was super human, such as teach the Pope to speak Latin, give advice to world governments on any crisis of the day, was special roving ambassador to Margaret Thatcher and was working on a global strategy to prevent world famine. This amazing daughter was also an internationally acclaimed actress and movie star as well as a global superstar filling stadiums with her distinctive pop modern and operatic capabilities! Malcolm also used to write letters describing his daughter's international escapades.

The present location now occupies a space not so far from its previous address in Kent Street. Bromsgrove Street, Hurst Street and Sherlock Street encompass it so it can't be missed. The current management team, recognising that very large venues, which this is, have changed such that now people seem to prefer the later-opening bars, have also purchased Angels Brassiere and Bar, serving food and has been developed to a very contemporary and high standard of excellence. I wish it good fortune. Wow, what a history from 1969 to 2011, moving from an almost secret society of back-street clubs to the fresh open air of true metrosexual life today. However, there's no more getting down to bingo with Laurie screeching out the numbers then shouting, "Well my ladies, lets get back to disco!"

*****

Alan Leighton and I at the opening of the Nightingale Club in Aston, 1975. Me in my 20s.

Dear Dennis and I, taken in 1969.

Deep in conversation with Dame Thora Hird.

Smiling with the Tog Master himself, Sir Terry Wogan.

In psychiatry, the beginnings of the idea of the 'therapeutic community' came from the developments inside the institutions. There were many famous ones that have gone into the history books, some of them are still in existence and although often threatened with funding cuts, some struggle to survive. The Henderson Hospital in Surrey has been on the brink of closure since 2007 and has unfortunately now been closed down. The Henderson was famous for its pioneering treatment of people with personality disorders.

The Retreat at York is still buoyantly going along. This once private hospital provides for the whole range of challenges of mental disorder and still adheres to its therapeutic community principles. Another surviving hospital is the Cassel in Richmond in Surrey, located in other sites before it became established on its present site in 1948. Originally, the hospital was founded to deal with shell-shock patients returning from the war - a luxury only a few were to benefit from. Its founder in 1919 was Ernest Cassel. It also became in full use as it had a principle at one time of admitting the whole family as the belief was that it is the family that scapegoat and create the tensions of instability and mental ill health. Just imagine how difficult that would be to achieve today with a complete nuclear family and the cost!

It was during those late 60s that I was introduced to these methods, working in your own, informal but smart, clothes using techniques of group and individual interventions. The construct of the ward unit as a family type of community where people would see themselves as part of a group and how both healthy and negative that can be in dealing with the world and relationships that people have to relate. These psychotherapeutic methods were well understood by some, mocked by others and practiced to effect for many. Unravelling the mind, getting feedback, dealing with emotions and not just talking about the weather, it could be a frightening and exciting proposition for both patient and staff. The social model that this was set in produced a far less institutional backdrop and could see profound benefits for some of the more insightful patients. These methods were the foundation of all talk therapies, yet provided in an atmosphere of availability and not some Victorian private clinic for the rich who were sent for the 'cure'. It was still the 60s darlings.

Later in my life's education, I studied hard to understand the more serious mental illnesses, but there is no better way to learn than by living amongst it and keeping yourself engaged. I experienced other specialist care, such as that that of mothers and babies and all that mental health, and the impact that it can bring, causing puerperal psychosis in the mother, impacting on a personality that before childbirth is functioning well.

Rehabilitation, or what is referred to now as continuing care. Criminality due to mental illness was always challenging. The area of forensic psychiatry was always a fascination and a risky game as those sometimes-clever psychopathic types were highly skilled, potentially dangerous and devious. That interested and challenged me.

Like schizophrenia, a thought disorder, and other major mood disorders, some of which I still lecture in and demonstrate for charitable and public bodies. These often-frightening disorders are dealt with in a more enlightened way but outcomes are never always satisfactory for many. You will read many a story here regarding some of those patients and the stories they had for telling.

Through all these early escapades Dennis would be around, making sure my needs were met, but still working hard himself. He was not so available with his time due to his working life. By 1972 he was general manager of the Mayfair Suite in Birmingham, the biggest venue for functions and entertainment for its time. If I needed to explode, talk, rant, rave or just sit quietly and if he was around, he was a constant source of quiet support, yet getting on with his own dedications to his work, often not arriving home until 3am after a large function at his venue. He would so often look exhausted and would eat on the run at his place of work, not a healthy combination but one he seemed to endure with relish - he was very much a workaholic.

Often we were like ships in the night passing each other due to my shifts and his schedules. It is always a strain when competing with yourself to be good at what you do. I think my personality traits were that of needing more attention. I saw, on reflection, that this mode of living was the start of my indiscretions.

*****

CHAPTER 6

In 1968, I heard an album by the singer Dorothy Squires and naturally Dennis didn't have much choice in the blasting out of her voice in our abodes. The former wife of actor Roger Moore, I was hooked on some self-penned songs - that album was named *'The Seasons Of'*. Dennis also had to endure my constant playing of this album. Eventually I added to that collection, so it must have gradually become more tolerated by him. He never complained and often said he liked her, but I secretly think not so much and so often when I was in a Dot mood.

I learned about her long career going back to a recording as a band singer in 1936 when she was a young girl. I met this great lady in 1969 and remained in contact throughout the decades till her death at 83 in 1998. Her behaviour and performances were legendary. I was invited to her mansion, St Mary's Mount, Wansunt Road, Bexley in Kent. It had been a former home of the writer Sir Arthur Conan Doyle, having acquired that name due to it once being a religious institution, so it must have had a few tales to tell and could have told many more through the times that Dorothy made it her magnificent home.

It contained 36 rooms and a swimming pool together with a gypsy caravan, which stood decoratively at the side of the pool. It was a present from an admirer, dedicated to a hit song of the same name. She had lived there with Roger after they met at a party at her home. She continued in residence there until that fateful day when it caught fire and she could have easily lost her own life after attempting to rescue her adorable dogs who lost their lives in this devastating fire. She was heartbroken.

This was the beginning of her ongoing troubles, with some 30 high court actions that she initiated. She was eventually to be declared a 'vexatious litigant'. In those later years, Esme Coles who lived in Trebanog in South Wales, gave her sanctuary and refuge in a house. This after leaving yet another temporary arrangement and partial anonymity, for a while at least, in a cottage in Ackworth Yorkshire. Esme kept a close eye on her, taking her to hospital appointments despite an often difficult relationship as they did truly care about each other. Dorothy had a champion at a time when she needed practical help.

By this time, Dorothy was not in good health, becoming very reclusive and self-isolating. At least I had good memories of happier times, both at Bexley and at Bray in Berkshire where she eventually moved to after the Bexley fire. In those fighting years, her candid conversations and her often not so well remembered kindnesses are remembered fondly. I still have an amazing collection of her records, now also compact discs, serving to remind me of her dramatic and often more sensitive melodic style. She had what we call the 'Three Cs' – Classy, Colourful and Courageous.

Dennis continued to be the ear of many of these developments with Squires, as my passion for her never diminished and he had to bear this recurring interest in her. He rarely ventured to any concerts she may have given, preferring to stay at home, waiting to hear more tales on my return, with food always prepared and ready. However, if she did appear more locally in those earlier days he would come along, though I never knew how grudgingly, poor soul.

Dot could be a firebomb. Unpredictable, yet to me I saw her sensitive side. In me, I believed she saw an unthreatening young fan who she knew adored her talents, but was not intending to intrude or enter her life like some crazed obsessive. I expected nothing from her except some understanding and some friendship if she wished for that.

*****

In the year before she went to live near Esme Coles, I wrote to Dot in Ackworth where she had bedded down and told her I was coming there, bringing Larry (Grayson) with me, and that we were not taking no for an answer. I gave her a contact number as I said she could call and rant but we were still coming! I told her clearly the day and time she should be expecting us. We had no phone call so on we journeyed. Dennis was used to these antics and knew well enough not to join us. His time, he said, was better spent doing things at home and not flying around Yorkshire looking for Dorothy Squires! With stage-struck theatricals!

We set off with a sense of intrepidity as to what we were about to encounter. Two younger men, who Larry knew, had done the investigation as to the exact whereabouts of this cottage in Britain's largest village. Once we were in the area they took us onwards in their car. On arrival we timidly went to the front door after entering a porch-type enclosure with a curtain over a glass part of the front door. I knocked. Nothing. I knocked again. Same non-response. "Try the door, get in." insisted Larry, pushing me on. Sure, it was open. I timidly stepped inside whereupon I encountered a pungent smell of gas!

"Dorothy?" I quietly asked, "You there?"

Slap on the back from Larry, "LOUDER BUNN!" Thanks for putting me in the firing line!

"Who is it?" came a bellow from upstairs.

"You know well who it is Dot! Tom and Larry as arranged!" I bellowed back.

"Down in a minute! Make yourself at home!" came the reply.

We looked around this dark area, split into two segments, warm and comfortable, with curtains pulled, allowing only a glimpse of light into the room. We could hear Dot moving upstairs. Doing a quick assessment of her living quarters, there were remnants of a nursing environment still present - a covered rubber ring to relieve pressure areas and to give support, together with a few other walking aids. Not Dot's as it happened. I could still smell this appalling gas.

Suddenly, bouncing down the stairs with a face scrubbed free of make up, wearing a full-length housecoat and huge glasses perched atop her gold white hair, she entranced into our presence with the words, "If I had known you were coming I would have got you something in". Well I won't go there - let's play the game.

She was in full flow, asking questions about our journey, worried that she hadn't even got us a glass of something in and food for us. I told her to sit and chat with Larry whilst I went to check on making us all some tea. As I knew she had that I got on with it, determined to check out this gas smell. Thank God it was an electrical kettle and we were all non smokers!

I checked through the cupboards as an excuse to find the cups, saucers and tea, but also to give me an idea of how she was looking after herself. I found the fridge moderately stocked with basics and essentials - obviously someone was keeping her supplied with a few provisions. I spent longer than perhaps I should, trying to track the source of this smell. Preparation done, kettle topped up and into the lounge area where she was engrossed in conversation with Larry. She was profusely apologising for her lack of preparation and telling me there were some biscuits, which I already had laid out as a good matron should!

"Now Dorothy, I am going to have to call the gas emergency services. Can't you smell anything? It's overwhelming."

"No Tom, I have no sense of smell. Besides, if it does I have probably got used to it. Well do what you think's best Tom." she acknowledged.

I got straight onto them, explaining quickly the desperation of the scene as I saw it. Someone was there in ten minutes. This young man came in through the kitchen, Dot out of sight in the lounge. As he entered he said, "This is a bad leak. I must isolate it quick." I stayed in the kitchen, not wanting to alarm Dot in the other room. He called me over after me reassuring Dot the problem was in hand.

"I have to shut all this down. The valve," he explained, "was hanging like a thread and was bellowing out gas at the rate of knots. I have to do it. Does she have other forms of heat?"

I checked. "Yes she had."

He told me his plan. Though not available now he would sort the problem by Monday pm. Today was Saturday. I went to inform Dorothy.

"What? Turn it off? I will freeze to death in this place." she screeched!

I said, "Well you have no choice. It's happening now so wrap up in blankets. Do you have an electric blanket?"

"Yes." she timidly responded.

"Good. Wrap yourself in that tonight in bed." I barked back, "Now I'll get this nice young man in to explain exactly what is going to happen."

In he came. Dot was carefully listening, gentle and very appreciative, as he told her, "Miss Squires (I had told him her name), this is serious and I will have the part for you no later than midday on Monday and I will promise you I'll return then and fit it and your supply will be safe and so will you. You do realise you could have been blown up - it was an exceptionally dangerous fault."

"Goodness me Bunn (she called me that sometimes), you have saved my life. My God, I had no idea. I could smell nothing."

She ran over, hugged me and held me - so emotional she felt like a little girl in my arms. After another short break for tea she asked how we had got here. We then told her about the two guys who were sitting outside who had tracked her and were waiting for us. "Go get them in, poor things. They can't wait out there." I fetched them in.

The younger man, although he had never seen Dot perform, knew all about her as he had great theatrical interests. As they walked nervously in to meet her, both did the pleasantries and sat down. I made more tea - once a hostess always a hostess! The conversations ranged from Larry and Dot talking about the old theatres they had known, laughing about some of those days and a few references to when, some 24 years before, I had been to Bexley. It was all becoming very showbiz with many a reminiscence, so I thought I am going to bring in some reality to the conversations in view of what had been in the papers. Dot was on her uppers so I charged in. "Can I just ask Dorothy how are you managing here with money and provisions, the bills and expenditure and the like. I want to know."

"I am fine Tom. I have my groceries bought in. Mike Terry comes to see if I am ok. I have my car hidden in a garage but I don't use it, I can but I don't go out at all. They watch me the bastard press. I never answer the door if I do, well you know, and as for money, there is no problem at all. I have everything I need."

True or not she looked fine and quite healthy in appearance, so why should I doubt her. At least food was in the fridge (even a half bottle of champagne, which I know she never liked). Continuing with her conversation, now to a full house, she turned to the young man and said, "Have you ever been to one of my concerts?"

"No, Miss Squires." he stated.

"You will!" Dot spat out.

Dorothy then would have been, by my calculations, 77 or 78. The evidence in front of us indeed proved to us that she could still do it! The time rolled on. We relaxed, so much conversation, then farewells had to come. She was so happy and relaxed and we also were, but it was now getting to a point where over five hours had quickly passed. We sadly bid our farewells, hugs all round, emotions, tears of joy and a wave from Dot behind the door so as not to be too exposed. Then we were gone. We were silent in the car. Larry and I looked at each other speechless - we were in the back as the two lads in the front were driving.

"Well duck, I am convinced she could do an hour no problem at the Palladium tonight. I don't seem so worried about her now." I said. We were relatively quiet on our journey, with our accomplices equally taken with this dynamic woman in their heads, finding it hard to believe they had not witnessed a broken down destitute woman. "Well she is Dorothy Squires darling." was my response to that.

Over the months Larry and I re-worked this visit in our heads to capture how she really was handling things, but we were reassured that the determination, pride and resourcefulness were in no way diminished. As usual, Dennis was given our stories of this recent chapter, both Larry's and my own detailed views of it. He showed interest and quietly stated, "Think of the life she has had. She has done it all. Why should you feel sad for her? She is comfortable, warm, safe. She doesn't have desire to live a life of dining out or gallivanting around. Think about that life of hers, she has done it all and besides she is an old woman. She will be fine." Takes a sensible man to know exactly how it is.

On the following Monday after 3pm I called her. She abruptly answered the phone, as often she did, sussing out who it was calling.

"Well woman, you had your valves sorted?"

She laughed and told me how wonderful and reliable the fitter was. How grateful she was, profusely overjoyed to see us and that was yet another memory. Though, as ever, a little more would come to Squires though it would be just a few more years before her life would end.

*****

Well eventual possibility of real eviction came and she had been offered a house near to Esme Coles, which Esme had standing empty. Esme contributed her own touching story that was broadcast at the time for a programme called *'The Slate'*, produced for BBC Wales. Dorothy Squires told her story to camera after some effort of persuasion by the BBC, telling how she became the permanent fixture and reclusive in that small valley town high in the hills near the Rhondda.

I had always said to her, "Look madam, you are a truly dramatic singer and Bassey (whom she had known), she is a truly theatrical performer and there is a distinct difference." She pondered this concept as I went on to expand on my meaning. Her emotive style of performance has not been matched, for me, by any modern day performer on a stage.

Despite several returns to that stage at the age of 83 she was admitted to the Llwynypia Hospital in the Rhondda under the name Edna May Moore where she died in April 1998. Much has been written about her over the years as well as Roger. It is documented regarding Dot's continual suing in the court amounting to around 30 cases and the ruination of her financially, that seeped away her fortune and resulted in her being named a 'vexatious litigant'. Well as often said, she did it her way.

I always thought that as she became older she was unjustifiably suspicious, resembling a late-onset paranoia that to some degree had been present in her personality. She would have been very difficult to treat and support for this, as I doubt she would ever comply or accept this possible diagnosis. She was not adept to viewing her life as a problem arising from her responses and interactions, as she had been a fighter and self-determined throughout her early life. She had been a woman in a male-dominated business. She was not about to change now. Besides, had she been susceptible to a little medication and compliance it may not have allowed the Dorothy we knew to be truly who she was.

It's possible though that she could have had a more peaceful inner life with herself, but I believe this is only hypothetical and to some extent I think she found more inner peace towards that end. She was, after all darling, only behaving like a star.

When Larry died on the 7th January 1995, we had a rare call from her as Larry and I had been up and demanded to see her whilst she was in

Ackworth in 94. She was furious that he had been allowed to discharge himself and said a man of that age should not have been allowed out so soon after the perforated appendix. Amazingly, it was Dennis who took this first call, and though they had only met on a few occasions she spilled and poured and spoke for a considerable time to him, with me trying to extract every word she had said from him. She gave a tirade on the phone for over one hour and launched into an attack of the care system, citing her experience when her mother was 'killed' by the hospital. Dot's mother had been admitted many years ago and she poured out the story to a bewildered Dennis.

So on handing over the phone from Dennis I continued to be the caller's recipient. I listened - it was all I could do, but she was very fond of Larry when she was a bill-topper in the 50s. Larry was often on her shows, small on the bill but great in stature, even in those days. Larry once told me a delightful story when he was asked to announce her on stage. Once, she noted his introduction as she stood in the wings and after the show she despatched her then young husband with an envelope as a thank you for his warm intro, it contained what was then a decent tip!

On another occasion she watched his act from the wings and as he wandered off she said to him, "Why aren't you a star?"

He said, "I don't know Dorothy. I always thought I was, but I might have to wait another 200 years!"

*****

Many a Christmas Day at home with Dennis and Larry was spent telling tales and sharing stories in the 90s about Dot and her early years, about life in general as people and friends do, particularly when Dorothy had been Britain's highest-paid female singer. As Dennis dished his sprouts, turkey and the trappings of a festive lunch, even he would be amused by the tales told. Even he could recall from his youth that stories were shared in a more positive light to an audience.

Dorothy had decided to write an autobiography by 1977 and at the same time went into the recording studios to produce the album entitled *'Rain Rain Go Away'*. The book was to accompany this. It was the first time that she had done a studio album for a few years. Many of her concerts having been recorded live in those days, first famously at the London Palladium in 1970 followed by many more. The album was a critical success, as it demonstrated her sensitive voice and style, reminiscent of her early career. Yet it still had the well-known dramatic trademark of Squires.

Within the book she wanted to publish some of the letters that Roger had sent to her. They included letters that his then present wife Luisa had wrote to him, which Dot had intercepted. Roger and Luisa went to court to obtain a temporary ban on publication of these letters pending a full-scale court case. The Moore's demanded the return of all letters and damages for alleged breaches of copyright and breaches of confidence. Dorothy characteristically fought the application saying she had been, "living and breathing this book for the past two years." Adding, "How could I leave Roger out of my life? It would mean skipping ten years of it." Continuing, she made it clear, "That in no way am I going to lose the respect of the public by writing anything bitter. I am not bitter. Roger has nothing to fear from the book and will realise this when he reads it. In fact my book will enhance him."

The eventual protracted outcome was that the judge ruled that, although she owned the documents, what was written upon the pages (the contents) were his. The book was never published in its full form, though a tabloid did print a serialisation, which Dot insisted they had not had permission to do. Another court case was pursued. Dorothy was quoted in the Daily Mirror that four months before she had phoned her ex-husband and offered him the opportunity of reading parts of the book containing the letters. "I wanted to put his mind at rest. I couldn't be fairer than that."

Years before she had stated, "I did not give up easily in my fight for the man I loved. But it brought me years of misery." I know that both Roger and Dorothy had many happy times. Dorothy was always working for him behind the scenes. Roger acknowledges this. Columbia were going to shoot the *'Ivanhoe'* series. They approached Roger. He returned to England, after acquiring an international stamp, to film the series at Elstree. During the week, he stayed at a small hotel, handy for his work, and if Dorothy was not on tour he would come home to Bexley for weekends. Dorothy had made it clear she was not the sort of wife to hang about the film set. Only occasionally would she drive back with him on a Sunday night and would have a meal out, otherwise she kept away.

Later, she returned to Hollywood and was there for the next six years. These were happy times, save for an incident concerning the actress Dorothy Provine who was the star of a series called *'The Roaring Twenties'*. Some newspapers were saying he was in love with her. One day, Dorothy just walked out and took a plane back to Britain and, no sooner had she arrived at the Bexley mansion, Roger was on the phone begging her to return - the following two years were some of the happiest Dorothy had I believe.

*****

I spent a memorable few days with her at St Mary's Mount in 1972. Dennis knew I was star-struck and was concerned as I was to drive there alone, well before days of satellite navigation and the like or mobile phones. He was concerned as ever and begged me to drive with care and concentrate on the journey in hand and to call him to tell him I had arrived safe. He was no way a showbiz type but was happy for me to see my interest in all of it. This visit of mine was before Dorothy flew to America again to prove her point there. I noted albums in her record collection that she had many male singers, but one artist that stood out was some records by Della Reese. I could see much influence in the phrasing of her songs to that of Della.

She cooked that night of my first stay. We ate in her large kitchen that had recently been refurbished. I was dined to stories of her time in Hollywood with Roger and the time she was over the moon to be in the company of Gloria Swanson and how she lived such a healthy lifestyle, and her belief in a healthy living. I know that Dorothy did some exercising and took saunas and had massage to keep her toned. Whilst I was staying there, she took a massage by a therapist who visited her at the St Mary's Mount home.

I was delighted to be given a downstairs study room complete with a comfortable bed. It was filled with memorabilia and black and white pictures, two of which I decided I must ask her for, which I did the following day.

"What on earth do you want those for?" was her response.

"I like them so much - can I have them please?"

My wish was granted. I still have those photos as a memory of that visit hanging at home. More photos for Dennis to tolerate no doubt.

It was a full year for Dorothy in 1977. The album, the book and a revealing insight to her in the Daily Express titled *'The Spy Who Loved Me'* by the famous no-holds barred journalist Jean Rook. Rooky had been shown a typical letter of Roger's, written hours after she had lost Roger's baby.

"I hope it won't hurt me to show you it." She was tearstained but not losing her composure. In every other way she was perfectly dry. She wanted to set the record straight. It had been said by many that he had used her but this was not the case. She knew he loved her and she wanted the world to know it at last. Jean Rook had thought she would do a 20-minute demolition job on her. She intended to pickaxe her stony heart. It was a harrowing interview, both granite-like and mellow. She bared all and it was a revelation on her temperament even stating, "Today I could pass Roger and that woman in the street without speaking. Before, I'd have attacked them. I have even retained my sense of humour. Parts of the book are terribly funny they will even make Roger laugh."

Will we ever know? Her story is one that would make a fantastic film. The first solo artist to hire the London Palladium to prove she was still a star, a fantastic night that was, for me on the front row, a memory many will have still. Yet again, Dennis had no interest in joining me - too preoccupied with his own work but was as ever happy for me to pursue my idealisation and interests.

Years later, in March of 1987, Dorothy wept after she was told by a judge of the high court, Mr Justice Mann, that she should be declared a 'vexatious litigant'. This is a very rare court move and even then she vowed to fight on and appeal to the House of Lords and onwards to the court of human rights. The evidence for the Attorney General, said at the opening of the case, was that she had, "Developed a voracious appetite for litigation." By this time in her life Dorothy had mounted 20 court actions since 1982. Nine of them being dismissed as frivolous or vexatious. It was at this hearing that the judge had been informed that Dorothy had launched a multitude of actions, ranging from claims of defamation, assault, conspiracy, piracy (of her autobiography) and fraudulent misrepresentation.

After the ruling Dorothy shouted, "This is not the end. It is the beginning! I am going to get my fans in their thousands and march down Whitehall." She wept and said, "I am livid. They have gagged me." As for that film, instant celebrity and reluctant investors and a project left too long can fade - it should not be allowed to. It would be poignant and funny and most dramatically entertaining, as was her life. Those of us who knew her miss her.

*****

Her funeral service at Port Talbot was accompanied by a Welsh male choir, which sang to a standing ovation. What a send off! Roger sent flowers but did not attend the proceedings in order, I think, to not overshadow this day. Some criticised this but you could never do right in such a difficult situation. She was finally laid to rest in the cemetery at Streatham where members of her family are buried.

Dorothy had been in conversations with Roger in those last weeks over the phone whilst in hospital. He had also paid for some previous treatment for some of her earlier cancer therapy. Since her death, he has funded a plaque in her memory in her former hometown. Perhaps time can heal many hearts and I still believed she always loved him and that he also had love for her. I think Esme agrees with that to.

During the last difficult decade, prior to her settling in Trebanog under they eyes of Esme Coles, she had been living in Ackworth in Yorkshire, not so far from Pontefract. She had gone to stay with a lady and her partner named Doris Joyce, a former night club owner in the north. Sadly, the partner of Doris had died and it turned out that she had never been married to him. Hence, the property that both Dot and Doris were now living in eventually became in itself a mine of legal problems because Doris became ill and Dot was helping her and nursing her. Doris was eventually to die of cancer, but the house became contested, as it had been owned by the deceased partner of Doris. Obviously, it had to be put in the hands of solicitors. The family involved with this were very sympathetic to the situation and allowed Dorothy to stay, attempting to be reasonable with the situation. However, it had to be sorted and Dorothy eventually had to go. Dorothy managed to get them to write a letter to say she would become homeless and needed help and I have a document of a newspaper cutting, which Dorothy used to highlight certain factors of her plight in order to strengthen her case.

Those ageing papers that I viewed proved she would have granted Roger Moore a divorce. These documents seemed to refute the claims that she wouldn't grant the dissolution of her marriage to him earlier than actually happened. The press in those days had a field day. She once said, "A Saint he ain't!" However, Sir Roger Moore is a true gentleman for sure, that I know.

*****

CHAPTER 7

From the mid 60s I met actors at the Birmingham Alexandra Theatre Repertory Company - we still had such things then. Through my associations I got an introduction and a pass to enter the hallowed gates of Associated British Pictures at the studios in Boreham Wood. It was virtually like gatecrashing the place to meet such luminaries of the time. Like my heroine Diana Rigg and Patrick Macnee, also raising a smile with guest star Peter Wyngarde who was to emerge later in my life when providing him with accommodation after reminding him of our previous meeting. This time he was to be touring in an adoption of *'Dracula'*. They were all a class apart to me - being in their company was exhilarating. It left a lifelong fascination for me with the minds and the talent of actors.

Wyngarde was highly successful at that time through the 60s and he was the lover of the talented actor Alan Bates, a well-kept secret outside of the acting world and show business. Peter was the most unlikely kind of heartthrob, but for a generation of women they swooned for the considered, camp, sophisticated, slick, charm of his character. An adept player in the title role of those hugely successful series *'Department S'* to be followed by *'Jason King'*, those iconic classics of the 1970s - still highly entertaining today.

Peter always travelled with a photograph of Vivien Leigh. He had a liking for iced claret and his main companion was his large Afghan Hound named Jason, who resided for periods in the back seat of Peter's vintage Bentley Continental. The time he was with us the hound sat and lay patiently by Peter's bed as he slept. The wolf was a well-behaved dog, which slept peacefully in the attic with Peter. As ever, Dennis was on hand to provide unfussy food, himself and catering for all our needs.

Peter kindly signed those butcher's aprons books and pieces of paper thrust at him with many a shopkeeper coming from behind his or her counter to see him (at that time Dennis and I had purchased a glorified café bistro called the Bus Stop Grill). He signed these autograph books, aprons and scraps of paper and left us with an exotic and enormous display of blooms as a thank you for our hospitality.

It was shortly after this visit that he was forced to come out regarding his sexuality due to a zealous press and a small misdemeanour. His sexuality and dalliances at that time overshadowed his acting and professionalism - a thing that today would be a one-minute wonder and may even enhance a career. How ridiculous it all was. The year that this unfortunate time in his life occurred was 1975.

His appearance in the now cult classic 1980 film *'Flash Gordon'* was ironic in that, for such a starring role, his face was covered in a mask as the evil sidekick to Emperor Ming, played by Max von Sydow to Wyngarde's General Klytus. Peter's unmistakable actor's voice was an immediately recognisable feature to me and Dennis, without needing to look at the end credits.

During the few years I knew Peter I did suspect that he had been a major influence over the actor Alan Bates. He didn't really develop much conversation on the topic - he was quite a private man. Peter to me was a sophisticated, charismatic and educated man who was able to use his skills and personality to fascinate - it came over as quietly powerful. Bates was often a more conflicted person, as actors often are. Insecure perhaps, he was more in turmoil with his inner-self in those social times. No doubt, at that time when Wyngarde and Bates were together, Alan was less secure and more vulnerable, perhaps more passive in his dealing with Peter. Some have said that Peter probably had more of a Svengali influence over Alan. Perhaps that was his choice. I am led to believe that Alan could not always assert in making his own decisions and choices. Whatever the facts, the relationship they had together lasted a decade from 1956 to 1966.

So my second meeting with Peter was at least eight years after the ending of that relationship. However Peter, as said, was charming, cool and presented, relaxed and in control - the mark of a bloody good actor. I have no idea where he lives but in those times he had a most pleasing home in Holland Park and a country home in Gloucester. Where are you Peter? I did hear that you sometimes attend the memorabilia shows at the international convention centre? Peter today is an amazingly well-preserved older man who still oozes his natural charm, smart and shaven-headed he looks younger than his years. Come back Peter we want you.

Diana Rigg, as we all know, went on to be the international dame she deserved to be. A classically-trained actress who in her mid 20s became the best loved face of *'The Avengers'*, the long running series then. Certainly a step up the ladder, both as a hugely-recognised star and eventually from earning less than £100 per week as a Shakespearean actor at Stratford upon Avon.

She was one of the last generation of actresses to sign a seven-year contract in Hollywood but returned to her theatre roots after that. By then she had given up her green Austin Mini, complete with a record disc player and probably now a well redundant motor - those ashtrays won't ever need emptying again in that overflowing car. I know from fellow actors who have known her far better than me that she is a truly lovable, gossipy sweetheart and well liked, formidable and fun.

*****

By the mid 1970s I had been a charge nurse and had started gaining experience as a teacher and clinical tutor, yet also working as a semi-professional in the clubs, pubs and hotels - in fact anywhere they would have me. I was known as Bunny Thomas, a comedy performer, singer and Mega Wreck! Again, Dennis was always there to offer practical support and tolerate this new found dual career. Dennis was also amazed by this unusually unique performer, but at this time no video recordings were able to be done and Dennis was always plodding with his work, so on arrival home he would have me to contend with, relaying what I could recall of my act!

My own foray into this unpredictable business had begun with me wearing a red leotard, an apron tied around the waist and large floppy rabbit's ears with a bushy tail, complete with my own shocking black hair, beard and moustache! I often entered the stage with cabbage in hand, unbeknown to the audience that on its leaves were the cues of written gags with other tips and mind joggers placed and secreted in other places - you see I had little memory even then! All this was well before the effervescent Kenny Everett hit the screens as *'Cupid Stunt'* in his series of extravagant mayhem.

I recall one show where, dressed like this, I raised some titters for sure, at what was in essence a stag show. I preceded the stripper, who never turned up, and as I agreed to go on the second spot after it had been announced the main attraction displaying his goods would not be forthcoming. After ten minutes into this second half, I was greeted with baying and bawling to, "Get your clothes off!" Really darlings with this body! I left the stage with the organiser offering me an extra £30 if I would go back on and strip!

"Get a grip." I said, "No way in front of that lot. I am a camp comic darling, not a stripper. I would be well under the microscope. No thanks and goodbye!" I flew to the car park as fast and as furious as I could, only half removing my ludicrous outfit, gasping with relief as I sped off in the car to my place of safety.

I was at this time still struggling to respond and learn my two crafts, which could provide some stable income, compared to the instability of so-called showbiz. It was like being pulled in two by a shire horse but my choice. As ever, Dennis was involved, quietly supporting me in the background, saying, "Whether you make it or not you will never starve if I am around!" They are both professions and both needed dedication. What was I to do? I was not about to choose by just carrying one and letting fate take its hand. Besides, why do things need to be packed neatly in little compartments? It was the mid 1970s and I was getting bits of cabaret work, but to meet the real world demands I became a tutor at the then Barnsley Hall Hospital near Bromsgrove. It was here that I met another lifelong friend Freda Perry. Do please remember the only thing that stopped me getting to the 'top' in showbiz was 'Talent'.

*****

Before all of this, I had met the now late, great Larry Grayson who became a dear close friend, often going on holidays and breaks over the following years. He was also adept at eating Dennis's cooking and enjoying his deserts and starters too. Larry was to spend his last four Christmas Days with Dennis and myself eating, snoozing, laughing and generally relaxing and just being all of us together having a cosy day and watching another Queen giving her speech. Christmas days for me, and many others, were never to be as much fun again.

We went on holiday to Malta at one time. We would laugh and gossip so much and be doubled up with laughter for such nonsensical applications of our minds. We would laugh at memorabilia and (tut) to be found in the tourist shops by the people we would meet, chat to or just observe as we meandered around or took an old bus around the island. We stayed at the Phoenicia Hotel in Valetta prior to its big refurbishment. One reason for the trip was for him to see an old friend from his home town of Nuneaton who had settled on the island of Gozo with his partner and they had a restaurant there. It proved to be a stormy, wind-blasted period and every time we were due to travel over to the island we had to cancel as no boats could sail. So the meeting for all of the week never happened. Only telephone conversations ever took place from the hotel room to his friend on the island. I don't believe Larry ever saw him again after that, but it never stopped us having some fun moments on the Malta trip.

Larry's heyday was as the host of *'Saturday Variety'* and *'Shut That Door!'* to become the highest-watched presenter with Isla St Clair of *'Larry Grayson's Generation Game'*, watched by up to 20 million viewers. Later was to be the beginning of the dearth of over-stimulated studio-presented want-to-be shows that we have all come to expect and to accept. Larry was to never audition in his life and as he often said jokingly, but not far from the truth, "It took me 242 years to get to the top."

He chose to live modestly by choice in a bungalow, one for himself and one for his adopted sister, next door to each other. Fan actually outlived him and before his own demise resided well in a rest home provided by him not so far away from home so he could go see her often. Poor Fan was to suffer from dementia with considerable memory loss such that often Larry would return with many humorous quips about her varying states.

"Oh dear Bunn, she thought I was Nelson Eddie and Jeannette MacDonald today."

* * * * *

Before returning to more about Larry and those wonderful times together, I am going to describe some more of the harsh realities and insight to the dynamics of a troubled mind.

I shall call her Maisie. She was a lady in her early- to mid-60s. She had had previous admissions to the hospital over some years. Her diagnosis was that of endogenous depression. This is a type of severe and distorted, almost delusional, mood disorder where the thinking is so dark and morbid it is far more serious than that of a more reactive milder type we may all be able to 'get our heads around'. Maisie was no exception. When she went to bed, her eyes would look sadly, as she muttered quietly to the ceiling so as not to disturb anyone else.

Full of doom and ladles of guilt she met me one early morning with her clothes a little dishevelled and that frowning look, with what seemed a permanent tear in her face. Softly spoken she muttered, "I mustn't stay here Tom."

"Why ever not, Maisie? What is bothering you?" was my reply.

"Well I am not supposed to be in that bed. I haven't paid for it and someone needs it. I don't deserve it, I must go to the police station and stay in a cell there. I won't take anything."

The look on her troubled, drawn face was heartbreaking but to her it was as real as could be. I distracted her to come and sit and have a sandwich and some tea, at least before she set out on her quest. Telling the nurses of her determination to go, I told them to observe her closely without being over-dramatic and try at all costs to dissuade her and to be with us. With another 21 ladies in varied states of mental health problems also needing our close eye, some established routine of a day to hold their interests for some time was required to dissipate those often bewildering array of symptoms. As some may say, downright madness.

Maisie pottered and disappeared to her room, leaving most of her limited clothing on another bed, placed as a present to be given to someone else. She was preparing her escape to the new destination when I asked her, though by this time not to the police station but to the public toilets. She said that was a more appropriate place for her to be as by this time she believed she didn't even deserve a police cell.

These beliefs in a woman with this diagnosis present a delusional morbid belief of bleakness and despair and to change this there is no instant cure or any persuasion tactics that work to change the thinking pattern. In many ways they are more high risk than the dramatic overdose type of threat, as often their belief in their hopelessness and worthlessness is so deep it carries a higher risk of intent. No matter how much you challenge, with rational logic, a person's thinking it will not change it. You must initially accept that that is the way they think. Morbid thoughts are horrid and persecutory. I have seen it so profoundly in others - it is both desperate and exceptionally funny to the person listening to the logic behind the thinking.

Well we managed as we did to keep Maisie, till one morning she had observed the change in shift changeover. Remember I often said to all staff at all times, "Our girls have all the time in the world to observe us and know our routines and where we are so watch out." Having just taken over the ward at 7am, ready for the day, I quickly scanned my beady eye and took a walk around looking for Maisie, whom I was assured was lying in her bed. There was no Masie there. I went outside and, in the distance, just ahead to be seen going down a long narrow path towards a more discreet exit in the grounds I could see her. Once out of the grounds, by law, I had no right to keep her, but if I could stop her I had the powers to detain her. "Sod it!" - she was on the main road. I jumped into my car deciding she would not be left to the cold elements or her own distressing delusional beliefs.

I was now technically a lawbreaker. I swung the door open with, "Hello Maisie! Good morning! So glad I caught you. Get in, I'll take you back with me."

She muttered, realising the futility of her flight with a few grumbles.

I said, "Well where are your clothes as it can be very cold sitting in toilets?"

She looked despairingly, "Well you know I am not worth the trouble. I'll be alright down there. Someone else needs that bed - they are far worse off than me." She didn't struggle, no energy to challenge my decision to return her to the warmth of 'Jane Austen' – no, not the dead novelist, the name of the admission ward from whence she flew.

Rolled up under her arm was a pair of knickers and corsets in an old plastic bag. Still some pride there I thought. Maisie was one of many characters who taught me all about the working of a mind that has been tricked into horror and despair which causes unimaginable anguish. It is still misunderstood by so many. Maisie was given food she didn't deserve, but was sat with a nurse who was given the task of ensuring she ate it. Even if it took an hour she was to eat it. This is just one small insight as all this would be happening in dozens, even hundreds, of scenarios around the country, often hidden away from the people who would fear it. A dozen more scenarios playing out in the arena of psychiatry right in front of our eyes. Truth is always stranger than fiction.

*****

A while ago, I saw a sad sight. Years before, when I had been a charge nurse at Rubery, I cared for a lady with the diagnosis of paranoid schizophrenia. She used to set fire to her bed-sit in order to get herself admitted to the safety of my ward. As she had been on many a section of the Mental Health Act it wasn't such a problem to effect another readmission but with certain restrictions. I used to allow her a lot of freedom when stable, knowing that life wasn't always to be simple because of it. This was down to my discretion as I knew that should things not work out she could be brought back by the police, should they be able to find her and they often did. She used to get on the bus and go to a café in Birmingham and she would most of the time return ahead of the deadlines I had set. One day she didn't return. She decided to board a train for a ride to London, making platform to platform and never seeing much other than the inside of a police car when her fare and obvious oddities came to their attention. So, restriction to the ward for around two weeks and the pattern would start again.

Once she wrote a letter to a local solicitor accusing me, the consultant and some member of the government of raping her. Well, due process and some sort of investigation had to take place! It soon was clear this was part of her condition. When I confronted her with this fact regarding myself she smiled with a fag on like a scene from *'Whatever Happened to Baby Jane'* and said, "Never, Mr Bunn, would I ever do such a thing. You are so wonderful to me." Showing her the letter she indicated it was a forgery and had not been written by her and swept away.

Some years later she must have been 'rehabilitated' in a community home. It looked awful to me, situated in Mosely, a suburb in Birmingham. I saw her trying to disembark a bus and as she struggled from it, her knickers just fell down around her ankles and she looked blank and disinterested and struggled on alone. She was dishevelled and not the 'Pam' that I knew with spirit and energy. I thought, "Well if this is community care, God help them all."

*****

It must have been in the late 70s when both Dennis and I were working very hard, with me travelling around clubs and the like - even going to Scotland once for a one-night stand (in a club darlings!). That weekend I had decided to drive Dennis, who had arranged a weekend away from his work, to stay with a friend who was living there in Moulsford Manor, which is in Wallingford Oxfordshire.

We started our drive and were well on the way when, abruptly, Dennis started the most powerful projectile vomiting I have seen. Luckily for us both out of the window, or when we had stopped. Knowing that this was potentially serious we turned the car around and after about another two major bouts of this got him home and called out the locum doctor as it was after hours. Even I knew there was obstruction. After an anti-emetic to slow down the vomiting he was sent as an emergency the following day by our own doctor, an old chap who spotted the problem immediately.

"Dennis, you have pyloric stenosis." This is where the pylorum leading to the stomach gets occluded (cut off) and creates these terrible symptoms leading to dehydration and other complications if not discovered and acted upon fast. Due to haphazard work patterns, late nights, food on the run and years of toil, he obviously had chronic peptic ulceration, as for years he had taken those white milky antacids to the point I thought he may turn into white powder himself. Well he was so weak afterwards but as soon as able, and looking gaunt as ever, he returned to his work as energetic and as focused as ever.

CHAPTER 8

Now a little more about Larry.

Returning now to Larry and the year 1972. I always watched those first shows of *'Shut That Door'* and on some occasions watched with Dennis by my side when he was not working. These programmes had sprung from his first big TV appearance from that live series called *'Saturday Variety'*. Like many, I was a big fan. He was truly a star made by the British public and not through a voting system of the now familiar *'Fanny has Talent'*. The public wrote in huge numbers to the TV company wanting to see more of this unique act.

For the viewing public he was camp personified, non–threatening, hilarious, a unique entertainer the likes not seen by family audiences before. He had made it at last. Not as erudite or as intellectual as Kenneth Williams but he seemed to reach out to the nation at that time. Not so amazingly, he ended the series topping the bill himself and, ironically, on that first live show of the series it was the return of singer Dorothy Squires. This after a decade-long absence from TV where she had topped the bill on that first Saturday night showing.

Our friend the late broadcaster and journalist Alan Leighton, who Dennis really appreciated and liked, took me to see Larry's first big production panto *'Aladdin'* at the Hippodrome Theatre in Birmingham. I was performing at some downtrodden working men's club at the time, as I often did, jumping at the offer to go see my hero give a masterclass in light camp innuendo and gesturing. I remember his entrance vividly (camp). He walked gingerly onto the large stage to a packed house, gliding to the microphone dressed as the traditionally attired Aladdin. He paused, gave his infamous glance in that Chinese style hat and stood, lips pursed, pausing for what seemed an eternity to say, "Do you like it?" gesturing to his getup.

"YES!" was the raucous reply, his retort being, "Mothercare", as he bounced off stage. That one word and his unique way of stating it was all it took to bring the house down - what an entrance. His familiarity won in just a short time through this appearance on TV had placed him in everyone's affections.

Afterwards, Alan said, "Come on, we are going back to see him." Alan himself was well known and a journo so we just walked to his dressing room, knocked and entered. After our introductions, Larry, staring into his dressing room mirror, said, "Look at this face," and pointing at the same time to his barred window in this basement No.1 dressing room, "they keep me prisoner in here for the whole run duck."

After a small gin and lots of chatter, we exchanged contacts and duly left to journey into the night thinking no more of any consequences of the encounter other than of a wonderful way to top off a perfect night. As usual, Dennis was never present at these occasions, preferring to work his socks off, his main addiction at that time. Getting the whole story relayed as always the following day.

I was amazed weeks later, the panto being a distant happening, to receive a phone call to thank me for calling around with Alan. "I did enjoy it duck." We conversed with more exchange of anecdotes and generally giggling and chatting about everything and nothing. He questioned me about my life. I told him about Dennis, a quick resume of life in short version, as he asked me about my intentions. Whether I would stick with the business or 'the other stuff', as I had told him about my health service occupation briefly. We just seemed instinctively to hit it off together as that was not a difficult thing to do with Larry.

*****

From then on, he would drop me little typed notes on his portable machine full of humour and gossip and I would respond in the same vein. Always telling me his plans and what was happening around his work - he was eager still in those halcyon days. Also, sometimes telling him briefly of my appearances around the Midlands.

I would later visit him in Torquay. First, he had an apartment there, then he decided to buy a house in the Lincombes after taking over the *'Generation Game'*. He made the decision to leave that show at his peak at the beginning of the 80s when, having obtained over 20 million viewers with the delightful Isla St Clair (more of her later), on a high. To think that he achieved those amazing viewing figures, a fact that his famous predecessor never did (not many people know that).

Enclosed are a sample of the letters that would arrive, always amusing, typed by him and signed in the name of some ancient music hall star or character. I wish they were still popping through my letterbox now.

After a visit I made to Torquay to see him, a short note arrived after he became aware of the death of a friend Michael. He had been tragically killed in his little sports car on Christmas Day 1985 after skidding on black ice on his way to work at All Saints Hospital intending to follow on to Dennis and myself after his duty had ended. It was a 'Looking forward to a slap-up Christmas lunch which was not to take place letter'. Pity it had to be written at all. Dennis was as devastated as me at this tragedy as he had grown to love Michael as a member of the family. Dennis had no resentment at this relationship and was supportive and often defended Michael when I was on my high horse.

It was 1979 when I met Mark and in 1980 through meeting Mark, I was to know Michael from 1980 until his early death aged 26, some six years later. I had met Michael whilst out with Mark, who was also to die prematurely in 1993. Dennis was party to all these comings and goings. Michael came into our house after knocking the door late one night, having been out clubbing with the aforementioned Mark who moved on with his life leaving the gate open for Michael to enter. He plonked himself down in a haze of Dutch courage and offered himself to me. He had to be pissed to do it. Needless to say, I did not take advantage of him as even I have a few principles - if only these things would happen today! This friendship would last for six years until the day of his untimely demise.

He is affectionately remembered and stored in the hearts of all who knew him and loved him. A feisty soul, funny, odd at times, a great companion and popular. He trained as a psychiatric nurse, with me as his tutor, and was well adored by his peers. Every Christmas Day in my heart he is with me as the timing of his departure was done for good effect and to last an eternity. He would have found that amusing in itself. What a day to go, Christmas Day. Is it the big bang theory?

Mark died much too young and I conducted his funeral by his request. Oh dear, do I have the touch of death? No, it's pure coincidence. What his family must have thought I don't know, as he had arranged the almost-humanist service to his own likes and it was from that day I committed myself to the idea of humanism as my faith and not to align myself with any historical religious belief system, with some God-like deity sitting at its pinnacle. Humans create all the difficulties in the world so it is only faith in humans to redress the balance. As I see it many of the corners of the world I have visited there is no evidence of any god having ever been present. Only in the minds of the oppressed in order to give them hope of a better life and indoctrinated into a historical myth created by men for powerful ends.

My impressions of some countries in Africa for example is that God, whomever this may be in our minds, has never made inroads to the minds of its politicians for any length of time to stem the corruption that blights the ordinary people who have to survive the best they can. Despite being sold the notion that education is essential for progression, it seems to benefit the very few. Faith and hope are an amazing sight to see in the poor and disadvantaged where religious institutions indoctrinate them even more so into their cults and hold them there in fear and damnation should they stray.

*****

It was around the mid 80s when Larry decided, "Fan (his adopted sister) is going funny down here in the winter. I think I'll move back to the Midlands." Hooray! I will see more of him and I did, with me flying over to his bungalow at every opportunity. Dennis rarely accompanied me, he was still bound to his work, and was always happy seeing me doing my own thing and always sent a well-meaning, "Give Lal my love."

When I purchased a new home in Acocks Green for Dennis and myself, Larry was the first over the threshold to view, nosey around and make his comments. The builder had just left so it was empty, echoing and sparse and looked so large.

"Well Bunn, what are you going to do with all this space? You never need it."

Larry Grayson

Alice's House
Nob Hill
Fakenham
Herts.

Dear Viola Tree,

Phoned sevarel times, keep forgetting you
are a working girl and have more important things
to do than just looking beautiful and dragging in
and the like.

Mae arrived safely, played it three times, I think
she looks marvellous when you think of the age but I
wish she had'nt have done it, lovely for us to see but
glad it was'nt shown in the cinemas.

Hope I can make the 16th, sure it will be great
fun and will do wonders for your new picture, do wish
you had'nt done a cowboy film though but you always
think you know best so get on with it.

Shall hang on to Mae's cassette until I see you
without you want me to send it back for others to
see, let me know.

Springs a little late this year (I used to sing
that on the clubs years ago) we get better weather
than you but still very cold.

Keep warm and do rehearse more.

Yours until the curtain comes down

Norma Desmond

Some examples of Larry's letters he sent to me through the years. How funny and
personal to me.

Larry Grayson

Alice's House
Lullaby Lane
Fakenham
Herts.

Dear Kate Carny,

Glad you are alright, loved your picture
but thought you looked like a man.

Recorded the TV TIMES AWARDS last Friday, had
a super time and the party after..WHOW !!!
its to be shown on Wednesday Feb. 26th at 8=oclock.

Recording a new programme this Friday called STAR
QUOTES, don't know owt about it so we shall see, my
dear friend David Clark (who does Looks Familiar)
is doing it so I don't care, nuff said.!!!

Do first dry run for one of a new series written
for me this Thursday, if I like it and they like it
then I shall record 13 half an hours during the sum=
==mer for next Autumn..hooray !!!

Must away, lots to do and have a
friend arriving at 12=40 for three days stay, its
all go.

Take care

Winter seems very long this year.

Larry Grayson

13/2/87

Cascade
4 Harcourt Gardens
Nuneaton
CV11 5UR
Warwickshire

Dear Tessa Thrust,

Hope you had a happy time in Germany.
I was sad when the Pantomime ended, I did enjoy
it very much indeed.

Returned from Torquay last Weekend, weather
awful but same everywhere, awful winter, lets hope
spring wont be a little late this year.

Shall be back in Torquay sometime but not for a
few Weeks I guess, from now on write to me here
at my sisters bungalow.

So nice to see you and your friend at the
Panto, wish I could have had more time with you.

Hope to see you sometime soon.

All the best,

Larry

One comedian being touched up by another. Joking around with Larry Grayson in his bungalow.

I told him to worry not, it would be full of my ego and room for his also.

It amused me that Larry's bungalow was named *'Cascade'* - just like his personality pouring out and a reference to a musical and film he knew. His previous house was named *'The Garlands'*. I wonder why!

My constant memories of him are always simple ordinary things producing belly laughs between us, often with Dennis at home making us snacks or meals, drinks and generally talk and view a programme we wanted to see on the TV, resulting in some scathing comments or laughter.

Dennis also loved Larry and Lal loved him. One Christmas Day I opened a gift from Larry. It was a biography, a large one of Marlene Dietrich by her daughter Maria Riva. The inscription on the inside cover read, "To my Dear Norma Swanson with love to Max. Love Larry."

One day we were walking down my local high street and deep in conversations as always. He would look up, look around at what was in his sights and remark, "Look at her love", whilst looking at this woman with a large posterior and hair like an exploding mattress, fag on and tattoos, wheeling a brat in a pushchair. He said, "There really should be more full length mirrors in this country. You can see why I gave up showbiz Bunn. How can you compete with that?"

On another day he was at the Flint Green Road house getting his coat on at the same time as staring intently at the TV. Dennis, for once, was at home and watching this as well but from the comfort of his armchair. Larry became more transfixed with a local news feature unfolding, reporting that a kid had been expelled from his junior school due to rude, foul, vile behaviour. Bringing into the feature the two sides of the argument the item cut from teachers to the brat's mother and dealing with the questioning. When the mother was on screen the child was swinging and running around noisily in the foreground being vile and loud with her demanding that he should be back at school and demanding he should be returned to class.

The other side of the point was dealt with by the headmistress of the school insisting he would not be allowed back to them and returning was not an option due to his constant difficult and out of control behaviour. Larry, transfixed at this debate with tempers rising and the mother standing like a harridan with a fag on, stood pointing at the screen in silence and bulging eyes and screamed, shouting at the screen with his own commentary, "BACK A LORRY OVER HIM!" Well he burst out laughing, as I did at these remarks.

*****

He would often talk more about the artists doing the rounds, mainly not big names or known from the past, like the Flying Reno's, The Fake and an old actress in the 1920s who just wasn't getting to the top. As she sat in the old fashioned rail carriage pissed in the days when these train coaches had doors each side of the carriage and no corridor she opened the door on to the track whilst the train was still moving, fell onto the railway line and eventually had to have part of her leg amputated. Well the way only he could tell a story was concluded with this: "Well duck, you see with all the compensation she got, it put her back on her feet!"

The Flying Reno's, he said, had been a wonderful trapeze and high wire act and they were getting on a bit. He said you could hear her teeth chatter as she climbed up the rope to do a twirl and foul expletives coming under her breath as she performed her routine with her even older husband. Larry said, "Well you could hear the bones crack as they went on with her saying 'F***ing hell' under her breath and smiling to the crowd below!" We would bend double imagining this and doing the actions between us. As for The Fake, well it was a fake - almost seven-feet tall, this man went around the clubs dressed as a nun! Telling wartime stories of how he dressed like this to escape the Germans. He was a fake for sure and got away with this act as most of the audience believed it.

We shared many journeys together, going to a few concerts in his later years and some pantos but the fun had gone out for this old trooper and he faded due to his own choice and was happy to do so. However, he remained a favourite in the hearts of the British nation.

He was due to return on the then exceptionally popular *'Michael Barrymore Show'*. Michael had been Larry's warm-up man on *'The Generation Game'* but Lal didn't make the date. Though this time, as we sat chatting in his flower-strewn side room, he was strangely eager to do it.

His discharge came from the George Eliot Hospital on the 6th January 1995 after a burst appendix operation. His manager, Paul Vaughan, helped him and took him back to the comfort of the bungalow. Paul was some years later to make a great gesture regarding Larry's memory. I'll tell more of that later. This early discharge, initiated by himself, left him in a state of collapse and internal bleeding at his home. He died in the morning of the 7th January that year. A sad loss to me and the nation, never to be replaced as a friend. How can they be?

*****

Regarding Larry's earlier performances it is now possible to purchase a collection of DVD discs of some of his performances that have been kept, whilst other have been lost or recorded over. Amazingly, only one surviving episode of the series *'Shut That Door'* survives with his last guest Diana Dors. There are the LWT specials and series on this set. It includes featured documentaries of life at home with Fan, presented by Janet Street Porter, together with other amusing outtakes and features of his memorial tributes and antics. Those were the times of TV for me, too often forgotten yet not so long ago. Well nostalgia does have its place. We all can continue to develop and learn from the past.

These TV productions became expensive and, some say, out of fashion. Well we all know about fashion - it all comes around many times dressed in a different guise. Those Stanley Baxter shows also confined to history but pulled out again when we really need a laugh and a trip down Memory Lane. Those productions of Stanley's became so expensive they became prohibitive to make. These remain in the minds of a certain generation who are still around and kicking. Well, depends how long this tale has sat on your shelf.

Today at least we are blessed with the often-cringing spectacle of *'Fanny's Got Talent'* and we must not forget *'The Sex Factor'*. Do I sound bitter? None of it. Humiliation was never in Larry's frame of reference, unlike today's so-called variety spectacle of bewildering talent shows.

*****

CHAPTER 9

Thinking of losses, I seem to be very experienced in attending funerals. Well you do if your friends are older. This reminds me of the funeral of Noele Gordon in 1985. This was captured as we left the Birmingham Cathedral for the national and Midland news on that day. I attended that with Larry who was a friend and they had appeared together both on *'Crossroads'* and in the theatre when he insisted they get her to star alongside him at the Palladium in Grayson's *'Scandals'*. They had maintained a contact and mutual affection ever since. It was a fitting tribute to a well-loved person who loved being who she was and the funeral was attended by many people who knew her.

Su Pollard was excited to see old friends and, so as not to interrupt people in her pew, she clambered over them to speak and chat to friends prior to the service. What a woman she is, a true individual. Pat Phoenix, who was an admirer of Noele's, sent a fitting tribute, apologising for not being there in person as she was a jobbing actress and was working and that Noele would surely understand. To think that just over 12 months later she was also to die - another much-loved British actress.

Larry was to indicate his thoughts to me that on her sacking from the new franchise, now called Central TV, she had deteriorated and ill health had followed. He always believed this to be the onset of the terrible cancer that took her life. Once, he phoned her whilst in the Priory in Birmingham and she was weak and in poor health. They put him through to cheer her up and his comments to her like, "I hear you have taken to smoking a pipe now" caused such belly laughs she was in pain and had to end the call through exhaustion. Larry was truly saddened as we all were - it was often said that, "She was Crossroads".

*****

The year before Larry's death I had heard that the actress Jean Fergusson was doing a self-penned play on the life of Hylda Baker. I took Larry as a surprise to see this production at Oldham. She was and is magnificent. Larry had met Hylda years before at the ATV studios in Elstree. Jean had this amazing ability as an actress and an incredible resemblance to her character, despite being much taller than the diminutive Baker. Jean had cleverly had larger props made to give the illusion of herself being smaller and also performing with a well-hidden stoop. Jean's ability to convey humour, pathos and Hylda's talent in this wonderful piece of theatre was stunning.

Jean also penned a biography called *'She Knows You Know'*, her well-known catchphrase of her variety years. It's a wonderful read for people who remember her or not. We met Jean after her performance. Also there was Paul O'Grady who was known before due to his incredible portrayals of Lily Savage that bought him to national prominence, who has gone on to do wonderful productions and seems a permanent fixture of British life on our screens - to brighten our days for many years to come I hope. When I met him, he was still performing his alter-ego Lily Savage, which he had perfected over many years, working hard all over the country and was awarded the MBE in 2008. Jean and myself remain friends and in contact today.

Despite her long-running series *'The Last of the Summer Wine'* ending, she will never be forgotten as the vamping Marina on her sturdy bicycle in short skirts and outfits. She will no doubt go on to many other projects as this lady is a great character actress and I could see her as a main character in *'The Street'* or *'Emmerdale'*. By the time anyone may plough through this she will already have played a character in *'The Street'* through the December period of 2010 and into the Christmas edition so it will be old news to the readers. So come on producers and directors get her in there!

It was shortly after Jean's book regarding Hylda had been published that she was asked to present a tribute and to interview Pat Coombs and Peggy Mount, two stalwarts of the TV, theatre and film industries. This took place at a beautiful little theatre in Newbury, Berkshire called The Water Mill. Sadly, by then, Peggy had virtually lost her sight and had been the victim of a series of strokes leaving her unable to be on the stage for a lengthy interview and tribute, but she came to be there that night and sat to tumultuous applause from the crowd and did make a few responses when needed.

Pat also by that time had been diagnosed with osteoporosis and was an active campaigner for that cause, raising huge amounts of money for research. The evening was a delight and ran smoothly by Jean. She showed clips of their films and TV appearances, some of them working together, and discussed the making of those times and the successes they had both had. Together with outtakes and clips on a screen at the back of this trio, a great story of two great careers unfolded. As a guest of Jean, it was wonderful to spend time in the company of Pat Coombs. She was painfully thin but looking wonderful and was so interested in all around her, including me. Jean sat with us for a while and we discussed many things that night, including my friendship with Larry who would often phone her for a chat to tell her how wonderful her appearances were in *'Eastenders'*. They would gossip at length and have a great old giggle.

Amazingly, after Peggy moved to Denville Hall, the home for retired actors, as they were such good friends and both alone, Pat decanted from her flat in Harrow on the Hill and decided to move to Denville Hall herself to be with Peggy. The roles that Pat often played were as the downtrodden female under the thumb of a dominant other character, yet neither of these ladies were really anything like the roles they portrayed. Peggy Mount was to die in 2001 aged 86, whilst Pat survived another 6 months and died at the age of 75 from emphysema. Both women had decided never to marry and as Peggy had mainly played battleaxe roles all her life and Pat was the one who was the opposite in acting mode, both fine characters, performers and talents who I am sure will be remembered for years to come.

Like most actors, Jean is a seasoned stage actress and she has done much work in many forms of the art. There will be stage TV performances awaiting her somewhere.

*****

In the late 1970s I often went to The Grosvenor House Hotel on the Hagley Road in Birmingham, quite often with Dennis as he enjoyed both the ambience and the food there, especially for Sunday lunch. Many a theatrical would pass through, those visiting to appear or whilst touring, some of them living in the area like myself. Noele Gordon, Danny La Rue,

Tony Morton (the original chef in the *'Crossroads'* series who lived locally) as well as his successor, the actor Angus Lennie, who had a soft spot for Dennis. People like Frankie Howard would visit or stay there when in Birmingham. Danny was often there with Alan Haynes, a great dame of panto who had a club at that time in London called the called 'The Havana'.

Both Alan and another performer Terry Gardener, another great comic and drag performer, were a double act in the 50s, being amongst the most successful and highly-paid pantomime dames of their time. Alan was to die aged 90 in 2008. Alan often appeared with Danny over those years.

I was once entering the door of the Grosvenor after a one-night stand, no not a guy, a club. The door was made of toughened glass, when out of a taxi wearing a Russian-style hat and beige coat and gloves and looking perplexed a man came stumbling by. It was Charles Hawtrey. He proceeded to walk straight ahead in an oblivious state, bouncing into the glass door and bouncing off it as fast as he had hit it. Dazed, but completely unfazed. The anaesthetizing effect of alcohol is amazing - that's why so many drunken people who fall have no pain at all when sustaining their injuries.

This well-known character actor, due to his legacy of the *'Carry On'* films was a man with a lot of bitterness, covered by his consumption of drinking. His disappointments by then had seen him undertaking tours playing the most unusual scenarios like the fairy Snow White. He was ensconced in the home that had once belonged to his parents in Deal in Kent. He was a notorious character there and his exploits well known. To think, like Thora Hird, he had worked on films as a juvenile lead with Will Hay.

Charles had never felt valued or taken seriously but his appearances in those camp exploits in the *'Carry On'* franchise were richer, funnier and magical because of his inimitable presence. He was to dig his heels in over a billing issue on one of the *'Carry On's* and wouldn't budge, so never made the movie believing they would succumb to his demand. But as we know, no one of that almost repertory of companies had a top-billing star status as all were deemed equal and besides, mayhem would be let loose in contractual terms, not as any of them were paid a decent rate for each movie they made.

Charles was the opposite to Kenneth Williams in matters of the private life, whose sexuality was an obsessive intellectual one of the mind rather than of the physical. Whereas Hawtrey would be outrageously flirtatious and engage in the most lurid of situations if he could get away with it. He could, especially if he had been drinking, even on set, lure a worker to his dressing room for some flirtatious moment.

*****

Jackie Carlton was an excellent, experienced northern comic I worked with on two occasions. He had won a top talent show after many years of experience in the business. He was again another unique artist who appeared on the likes of the then popular TV programmes such as *'The Comedians'* alongside others like Tom O'Connor, Bernard Manning (the one we all loved to hate together) with George Roper and others.

He was at this time a direct competitor to Larry Grayson as he also had a camp style and effervescent, yet drier sense of style. It just didn't seem to happen for him in the big time. To pull that off you need a big powerful advocate to make it happen, so as a sustained TV entertainer it wasn't to happen, but what a great club trouper he was. He has a series of flamboyant sparkly suits, one made in zigzag patterns and a paisley one - most eye-catching to say the least. With his thick-rimmed black glasses and greying hair he was a sight to see. These suits caused a delight at the London Palladium, his pay off for winning the talent show I mentioned. It appeared Larry was the one to be favoured for regular TV exposure at that time.

Going to see Jackie if I got the chance and to finally work with him on a cabaret bill was an honour for me as he was always sensational. I adored his work - another artist who is no longer with us. Throughout all of these days, I was working away in mental health, yet working semi-professional as an entertainer.

*****

I remember, clear as a bell, having Sunday lunch with Dennis at the Grosvenor, always an occasion of flippancy, fun and people gazing with bitchiness and the out-doings of attention-seeking behaviours. Young and old queens gathered together with their mothers, aunties, fag hag friends and lovers - a real concoction of human life and playfulness. On this occasion, during lunch, the comedy performer, singer and actress Joan Turner (another bill topper of her day, having appeared on Royal Variety Performances and the like) began rolling down the bank near to the swimming pool, miraculously holding a champagne glass at the same time! It was quite a sight to behold. Even Dennis considered this a clever 'act'.

This was now 1978. I was to live through that period following her ups and downs, trials and tribulations, and watch her undeniable talent take its toll on both herself and that of agents and bookers alike. Although a lover of a few drinkies in those days it never seemed in any way to interfere with her performances and she could be very controlled when working.

She was warm, funny, serious and unpredictable but always loveable unless she was staying under your roof for one of her elongated stay-overs. Often I would introduce her on stage as she was still getting regular decent cabaret work. She was dissatisfied with the business, believing there was little place for her type of stardom. Due to this dissatisfaction she eventually came to the conclusion that she should take one last stab at America saying, "All my old mates are there, Tom Jones, Englebert Humperdinck."

In 1977, she had been declared bankrupt, mainly due to the Inland Revenue's demands, though her extravagances could also have assisted. She was determined to work through it to pay of these debts. The Rolls Royce went - well it was taken away. After reporting it missing to the police they were to call her back saying, "Miss Turner it hasn't been stolen, it's been taken away by the finance company!" Eventually, her three telephone lines at her mews flat in Marble Arch were systematically reduced but she clung to them as she would chat up the then collectors of debt at the telecommunications department, making arrangements to keep this juggling communication live and unhindered.

Over those years she worked and paid off those people at the Inland Revenue, the first to have to be settled with, and was eventually discharged. It did not sink her, she fought on in her own way, always cracking a wise snap at anyone she felt was doing her down in those past days of variety, but laughing at it all as she went.

She was partial to a few little naughty pleasures. Wearing a large, almost pillar-box red, swagger-type coat she would enter a local convenience store singing and interacting, being jolly and amusing, pay for her items and leave with a farewell and "ho!" - not knowing she had extracted an extra catch for the day. "Joan, how could you do such a thing?" Responding in a carefree manner she would say, "Well mother's coming to tidy the flat tomorrow and she loves a bit of chocolate and besides, they have so much they won't miss a little bit for mother." Mother was 80 years old then. She was naughty, almost little-girl like and would relish telling me her exploits (far too many to mention) that often involved gate crashing celebrity and charity events where they, "...had forgotten to invite me."

She did go back to The States, eventually being photographed in a double-page spread of her so-called demise in a daily newspaper under the headline story, 'DOWN AND OUT IN BEVERLY HILLS.' That was our Joan! Pictured posed, but defiant and still resilient, as looking gloomy and despondent with a large black plastic bag at her side claiming these were her only possessions. Clutching a few photos of her contemporary stars and friends, together with a video of her on her last appearance as special guest on the then popular *'Michael Barrymore Show'* where she bought the roof down once more. Still insistent, having even refused the offer of her family to return the UK, she sparkled and stated, "It's so cold and drab there I am better off on the streets of Los Angeles than being on the streets of the UK, particularly in Streatham." Streatham was where she was encouraged to go. She was to eventually return.

With many more anecdotes of her later life, years later she was holding court at the club for Acts and Actors in Covent Garden. Frequenting this, one day some people bought her some copious amounts of fluid and she somehow urinated over her chair. It was duly sent away to be cleaned and made good. On its return the club manager christened it the 'Turner Prize'. Linda La Plant wrote a fitting tribute about her and did give her work. She recognised within Joan her qualities and character, that gave joy and spoke fittingly of her naivety and endearing quality.

In many ways, in showbiz, Joan was legendary and had a most colourful career. Her one-woman shows were blessed with a great sense of fun, a voice which could produce operatic arias, impersonations and a variety of jokes always raising hilarity wherever she appeared. She was often referred to as the woman's answer to Harry Secombe. She was one of those old timers who had the knack of making everyone feel like they were an old chum.

Her first professional appearance was in music hall in London at the age of 14 and following that she toured in review. Her talents were soon spotted and she went on to appear with the legendary Crazy Gang at London's Victoria Palace and the London Palladium. She played all the leading venues and theatres of her day. She was chosen to appear at the Royal Variety Performance, and in the later 70s was acclaimed for her Silver Jubilee Performance. She had a famous four and a half octave voice. She was a good actress, able to surprise audiences of the time with her portrayal of *'The Killing of Sister George'* in the London theatre and then the provinces.

She also turned in a few performances as Auntie Lou in the series *'Brookside'* though that didn't last so long as her old-fashioned questioning of her character and role didn't rest well with the tight-running scheduled format of a 'get it in the can' series.

In 1991, she was the winner of the Manchester Evening News Drama Awards as Best Supporting Actress. She turned in a few cameo performances including the nosey neighbour in the film *'Scandal'*, the story of the Profumo Affair. It was a well-received movie; her part was miniscule but she could still light up the screen. It was after this that she became very disillusioned and reverted to some of her old addictions and decided to get off to The States but I took Larry Grayson to see her one last time before his death at Oldham.

I wanted Dennis to come with us, but he declined, preferring the comfort of home to yet more theatrical encounters. It was a surprise for Joan. She was thrilled to see Larry and myself at the ending of her show. She was of course wonderful, giving as well as her comedy portrayals, her interpretation of *'Send in the Clowns'* in a heartfelt rendition sitting in front of the footlights, Garland-like fashion - a most endearing scene that I watched performed on many stages over many performances over many years.

She could recreate an atmosphere of joy with her uncrushable sense of fun, making people beg for more. You could never ignore Joan - even when down and worse for wear her talent could still win you over. Pity that often she was overlooked when she needed that guiding hand at those times, but it would never have been easy I know. I too tried often when there had been some drama or fall out. I would discuss or try to get

her to look at her part in the scenario. The lovely, talented Roy Hudd can tell a tale or two about Joan and refers to her in his books. Particularly when she was appearing in the West End in *'Oliver'*. It's a story often told and has passed into showbiz history so I won't tell it! Though she did tell Cameron Macintosh where to put Oliver's bowl! Goodbye West End!

Once she was staying over with me in Birmingham and she had overstayed her booking by around one week, as she often never knew when it was time to be called. Dennis joined us on some occasions and liked Joan but knew instinctively she was hard work. But they got on well. We went out for dinners and sometimes even Joan contributed. She once bought me a wonderful tie for my birthday. It was elegant with polka dots. Oops, I do hope she paid for it! Yes she did. I recall clearly driving back to her place at Marble Arch and as we drove on, I was attempting no doubt to guide her in a direction that would be helpful as she turned to me saying, "Love, I know you mean well but I am to old to change. All I have is my talent."

She arranged to take me and my friend Michael for lunch before she caught her train back to London. Well 2.30pm came and went and it had taken her all morning to scrub up to star status. We arrived at the station and she checked her return, only to find there was no refreshment buffet car available. She said she wouldn't travel on this, as how was she supposed to survive to London without 'refreshment'? Our lunch consisted of a beef burger on the concourse and a letter being mentally drafted to Sir Peter Parker, the then chairman of British Rail, complaining about the lack of services on that Birmingham to London train. Waving goodbye to her, I was left with the feeling of joy, exhaustion and the giggles, she clutched her bags and set off, Carmen heated rollers ready for her next adventure - there were many more to come. Joan died in March 2009. Let at least my generation and the previous one never forget this extraordinary bright light.

*****

CHAPTER 10

I have had two important Fredas in my life, one briefly mentioned earlier. One being Cook, the other Perry. As for Freda Perry, she virtually ran that school of nursing in Bromsgrove as I said. On my first day there I thought she was chained to her typewriter and said so. All were amazed when I took her to lunch, as she would often just make a cuppa and work through. I was soon to learn all the dynamics of this institution. I believe that if she had never been there not one student would ever have been enrolled properly or ever made the state final requirements. She was not always appreciated by the ones who should have known better, being surrounded by egomaniacs who were at constant war. Over the years, I have sent letters, cards, notes and photos to her and I discovered years ago that she has kept everything she ever received from me in an organised file. Revealing recently that some are so funny and some full of despair, I really should have revisited them for these pages but have not. She remains a constant support. We met around 1975.

My other Freda, Freda Cook came to us as housekeeper in 1985 and witnessed a lot of our unorthodox life. She stayed and moved with us to the two properties in Acocks Green. She was originally asked to come to us for three days each week - she came for five and did more hours than a pit worker! She said she preferred being here than being at home. She was a lifesaver for two busy guys doing their own thing and working hard. She did everything, unimaginable tasks. She was always on ladders and once I threatened to get her a job as a high wire act! Often joking with her when she had finished, that she must go outside and point the walls and straighten a few slates on the roof. I think if I had let her, she might have done. She is fit, well and happy with granddaughters and now 75. Good old Freda and you're still looking good, just like my other Freda.

*****

Jumping around in this scatty brain, the late 80s are now in my head. I was over at Larry's bungalow and we were talking about Bob Monkhouse who I had briefly met in the late 70s at a cabaret club in Stratford-upon-

Avon, called the Toll House. Bob, who by the late 80s and early 90s had taken on the run of the revamped *'Opportunity Knocks'*.

Lal (I always called Grayson Lal) was saying what a gentleman he was, a good man, the best comic ever. When he came on screen, his persona seemed like syrup to some. Yet he was the best comic talent of his generation and so very multitalented, which I think we all know. Larry was saying how he himself had never auditioned for anything in his life and was lucky to have been eventually seen at a time when the public and producers were ready for him. When Larry had been asked to judge people he found it really hard to watch them and it was often a humiliating experience. He considered himself lucky that eventually, though rather late, he had been discovered. He advised me, "Don't do it love."

Well I had not auditioned for anything in those years from the late 60s until now, almost 1990. I decided to 'secretly' audition and not tell Larry, who I knew would disapprove. Well I duly did the first round and the second and to my surprise was called back to the final one at the Riverside Studios in London. Stewart Morris was the producer and the finalists could bring three people into the theatre to create a live atmosphere in the audience. Two friends, Maurice and George, kindly accompanied me and I asked them to look at the TV monitors to judge for themselves how I came across on camera. For this audition Bob was present in the room and sat in his elevated position. He apparently attended the finals but was not responsible for the final say on who was put through. The programme has to get its quota of impressionists and singers.

I was the only comic on this bill. Well I did my five minutes of camera in a suit and gave it my best shot. Walking off to the dressing room I sat to reflect and the door opened and in walked Bob Monkhouse, my hero. "Bunny, that was wonderful. A real treat and reminiscent of Howard and Grayson, but your own stuff I loved it." He didn't have last say on the acts he told me, but not to worry. He informed me that Stuart Morris had to get so many acts and fit it all into a schedule for the format. He told me he wanted to write some material for me as well, and that I was to try it out and that he would keep in touch with me. We continued chatting while I was thinking, "This man had sought me out?" This was typical of his passion for comics.

The unmistakable hand of Bob Monkhouse. I treasured his letters.

After the whole initial event was over, I told Larry what I had done so he couldn't dissuade me. "Well duck, I told you. Why you put yourself through that? But isn't Bob a lovely man? Best you didn't get through love it could have finished ya."

*****

In the 1950s as a young child, my memories are hazy but I do distinctly remember seeing a funny old woman on the box or at least listening to her on the radio. I was very young. In later years, I was to clearly know who this 'persona' was. Rex, I learned, was a very private character and always appeared as the character Mrs Shufflewick, with no reference to his real name of Rex Jameson. Strangely enough, this character that he had created merged with the real life Rex as they were both in equal measures a boozy pair of souls all in one. His real name was Rex Coster, which I believe only surfaced when he died in 1983 on the completion of

At Jean Fergusson's book launch with the delightful Paul O'Grady, both looking a little younger in 1997.

With the late, great Norman Wisdom at the celebration of Larry's life.

Larry and myself outside his home with him clutching William, his last ever poodle.

With the great Dorothy Squires. She was 71 here and wonderful.

Taken some 12 years after we first met, with Joan Turner gossiping again and putting the world to right. "We clowns who choose to entertain."

With the wonderful actress Jean Fergusson whilst she was touring with her show *'She Knows, You Know'*.

Smiling with Su Pollard. She is always a laugh.

his death certificate. He rarely gave interviews and lived a somewhat hazy life on the edge of the mainstream. He was a puny character throughout his life, often looking frail and undernourished, somewhat tramp-like but he was magic.

Larry had often spoken of him, and when I met him one night in a haze he had been adopted by the London gay scene who adored him and his character. In fact, that's all they knew, the invention. His famous haunt to show off Mrs Shufflewick, many will tell you, was the Black Cap in Camden Town. He was always asked to go there, perhaps for a few quid and a few barley wines and scotch, or whatever was going. He had no worries being plied with the stuff. It was those last remaining days where audiences, even in gay clubs, would stand quietly to be entertained by this characterisation of this little old gal.

He was also another member in the 1940s of the Ralph Reader gang shows. Here, he really learned his craft. Many a list of comedians rose from this institution of the gang shows as well as the infamous Windmill Theatre of the pre- and post-war years - Bruce Forsyth, Peter Sellers, Jimmy Edwards as well as Harry Secombe. I am told it was a hard training ground. As the years went on, the character became more boozy and not so genteel as the early days. I admit I was heavily influenced by him and my own creation of Edith Shagpile was not a million miles away from him

but less boozy. More Women's Institute with a Midland accent, which is my own.

Although I occasionally saw him at the Black Cap in the later 70s, my conversations that are more memorable with him happened in Wolverhampton. On one occasion I took Dennis to see this talent and another time in Birmingham. It was those rare times when he ventured in his flat cap out of his comfort zone to do a provincial gay club or gig. This lone figure could be seen coming from the bus station, little bag in hand, literally shuffling towards his gig for the evening, and venturing back afterwards - if he could.

There was one place in Brum on the side of the Hippodrome Theatre, the name escapes me. It lasted around three years and was a nice building that had been a former church. Thank goodness it wasn't any more!

Again, I encouraged Dennis to attend this one, but he declined. Before he went on I popped in to see him. He was engaged in putting his make-up on very slowly and talking quietly through the mirror to me. He said, "They are writing this book about me." He was being helped by a young man called Patrick Newley, who had taken the task of managing him. Patrick, a journalist and stage-struck youth like myself, ploughed his energies to improve Rex's bookings outside of London - a risky business! Rex continued, "They keep asking me to remember things years ago (still stretching his eyelids and pausing to place on the make up). But I can't remember f***ing yesterday dear! Oh well."

After some more banter and some nice conversation, I hesitantly bought him a drink. I know I shouldn't have but what to do? I took my place in the audience. He was on form and was truly wonderful. Sadly, Patrick died recently far too young. His columns he wrote in *'The Stage and TV Today'* now simply *'The Stage'*, are sadly missed - a talent in journalism and showbiz in his own right.

As for 'Shuff' his ending was on the 5th March 1983, just short of his 59th birthday. The cause was stated as a heart attack. No one could ever have stopped dear Rex from drinking, I know Patrick tried. Rex's life had been one of continual smoking and alcohol, which diminished all appetite and played havoc with his vital organs. After a binge, he would often lay down for a couple of days, to recover to start over again. "I am suffering from whiskey-itis." he once told Patrick.

His funeral was amazing. It was thought that a handful of old friends would be present, but well over 500 people turned out. At Golders Green all those old performers, queens, comics and other fans who loved his work. Typically, he left no will. The Entertainment Artists Benevolent Fund Paid for his funeral. I think every poof in London was there. The cameras and press were of course more interested in the celebs who were there in attendance. In that amazing act of this old tart he had created, soft-spoken and hazy much like himself. He would end his act with, "I am going to pop off now and I'll tell you why. I've left a large whiskey in the dressing room going cold and I had one knocked over in 1927 and I still wake up screaming about it now." Well that was Rex.

CHAPTER 11

We all have sex lives and love in our life. And then there was Dennis. Returning to when I met Dennis in 1969, I was a relative newcomer to this experience, having met one black guy and shared my flat with him and others whilst a student. Who knows what love is supposed to be at 18 and still discovering my sexuality?

I did have what I believed to be a satisfying relationship with a fellow student named Lynn. We knew each other closely for a year or so. She was bright and educated and a considerate type. She even suggested I try a man and see what I liked! Well how could she know? So I did. Lynn and I are still friends today and she has been married and lost her husband some 20 years ago to a heart condition. As for Johnny, my black guy, that was to last less than a year. He was a mixed blessing but did confirm one fact - I was and am gay!

Meeting Dennis was to change and develop both our lives, as partnerships do. He was chef manager at the then Central Electricity Generating Board, in those days in a contemporary building in Shirley, Birmingham. I had met him on a weekday after daring to go into a gay club alone, a break from the work at Highcroft Hospital. The Victoria club was run by an eccentric character named Laurie Williams, again a man who I knew until his death.

In those days gay clubs, such as they were, gave an air of furtiveness and of the underground even though the law had been reformed to some degree the previous year regarding homosexuality. They seemed a safe haven at the time and this evening, Dennis, as I was to discover his name, was dancing very badly alone on a dance floor with about six others. I stood alone, looking unobtainable and shy - to some degree I was. He wandered over to me and fiddled with my St Christopher dangling around my neck and asked me to dance. Of course I said no. Instinctively, being shy, I knew how to play hard to get. He asked me to meet him the following Wednesday at a landmark known well in Birmingham, the Birmingham Post and Mail buildings in Colmore Row. Well I turned up and so did he. Many years later he told me he arranged that place so he could just get back easily on the bus and return home, as he didn't expect me to turn up. Well I moved in on his life for good and for bad until death it did part us!

We were both working hard, him in his catering and management work. He was 28 then and in his peak. I was still a student nurse and doing all the odd shifts we did in those days. For around four years, most of our lives were centred on home building, working all hours and me still trying my hand at entertaining when I could get a gig.

Dennis became General Manager of the Mayfair Suite in Birmingham, a huge function suite owned by Mecca. Under his leadership, he also turned the venue into a concert and entertainment venue, long before the building of the Night Out venue housed in Birmingham, featuring such artists as Rod Stewart and Hawkwind. It also hosted boxing tournaments and prestigious functions galore. In this era and in this venue were to be seen Edward Heath on a speech tour as Prime Minister and Enoch Powell delivering his powerful rhetoric to a packed audience.

One memorable occasion was a live broadcast of Pete Murrey's BBC *'Open House'* with special guest star Eartha Kitt, who spoke to Dennis and myself through large mirrors in his office and finding it hard to look us in the face. How strange I thought, but at close quarters, I believed she was so very shy. Dennis was quietly innovative and also ran jazz evenings with the likes of the wonderfully classy Elaine Delmar.

During these years I was often alone late at home, as Dennis would arrive back often after 3am in the morning and out again around 8am. I would get bored when not working or off duty and not doing my turn anywhere. I started to drift and though I never considered myself a slut, I did never hide the fact that I had others interested in me. Dennis remarkably never tried to stop my indiscretions, and always seemed to accept and even befriended some of these companions. He once told me he could never be enough for me. What can I say? I was to understand this more fully as I discovered more of his own damage in later years, some I have told you about in earlier pages. He had been the victim of so many cruel dealings from the nuns of the Father Hudson's Homes in Coleshill, Warwickshire, now as derelict as some of its souls who inhabited it. He rarely talked about his experiences as an orphan there but I was to discover its extent later.

He once described another graphic detail before his breaking-down incident, which I told you of earlier. How once as a little boy he was given the job of laying up the dining room refectory and dropped a fork on the floor. A nun took hold of him, put him between her legs and beat him repeatedly, a common occurrence for those 'angels of God' to let out their frustrated urges on their vulnerable little charges. I hope towards this end I did support and offer him something only I could do, to become his advocate for his physical and mental health. I was better than his early torturers and no matter how bad I may have appeared to have treated him, he felt safe with me even in my own often chaotic behaviour. He knew it was borne out of love. I wasn't always proud of myself, some of the ways I must have treated him, but I truly loved him and each day I miss him more. The saying time heals is a nonsense - it doesn't.

Through the 80s and 90s, he was the Director of Commercial Services for Birmingham University, turning deficits into healthy profits under his directorship and leadership, with his quiet serious way and intricate knowledge of his trade. He had many credits to his working life, respected for his hard work, this poorly, now self-educated man shone as a deep, hardworking dedicated pro. His natural intelligence shone bright. Late in the 1990s he was to be disposed of by the new cut and thrust politics and psychopaths that inhabit any new order. I was still sometimes engaging in other relationships spasmodically, some lasting up to three years within this triangle.

Dennis dealt with his new-found rejection of work by spending a few weeks at our house in France with me. He then returned to develop a small business we called Natural Kitchen, a vegetarian food production unit in Coventry, until he became too unwell to continue and at my instigation he gave in and became a full-time live-in carer and cook for me! Bless him. His own choice I'll have you know. I never was hungry in my life with the fantastic food he cooked to sustain my ravenous appetite, and that of my many friends including Larry.

*****

In the early days, as I explained, he had many positions in the Midlands, like his tenure at Mecca. After the Mecca years, he worked for one season for the official receiver in hotels and catering businesses with a view to salvage what he could of the business with a view of winding them up. One such venue was a large country hotel near Kenilworth. He pulled together what business he could salvage and functions that were a possible runner and delivered the goods with the staff who had been responsible for placing the business in jeopardy in the first place by ripping off the owners. At these times I wasn't seeing other people but as ever this was not to last.

Dennis was more than a match for these employees at this once famed hotel, placing large locks on the wines and spirit stores and stocktaking himself after a midnight blitz on the place with no warning. He was not popular with its institutionalised staff. On their arrival early for their own secretive raid on the stock he confronted them. Standing in shock, these takers standing outside the barred stock rooms not even knowing who he was. Game set and match! He identified out of the troops a couple who were happy to spill the beans. Now the game was up and they helped him provide sufficient functions still on the books to earn a few more months income and duly dismissed the rest and informed them if they returned to the premises they would be trespassing and in breach of the law.

I saw him in action over this period as I also had household bills to pay and drove over to stay some weekends in the Princess Anne Suite! To ensure he gave me the household income to prevent us going our own insolvent way! He could direct others pragmatically, yet was soft and firm in equal measures. You could see the respect others had for him. He was a guy who knew what he was doing. He not only could preach it, he could demonstrate that he was more competent than others who saw themselves as experts and who could talk the talk.

I witnessed him moving furniture, chairs, stages, organising the few leftovers of a workforce to help him rearrange function rooms, place things into elegant arrangements for clients who were paying the bills, thus reducing the hotel's debts. His sheer physical stamina and sole determination won not only my respect, but that of all who worked for him. He stayed on the premises, as he was also responsible for any possible return of the old retainers and their light fingers, so I would on some occasions stay over when it was possible to do so.

Even before these times we purchased an ex gas board van, signed it with Docherty and Bunn Caterers and, in-between our regular jobs, we did events. We could hardly manage. From dinner parties for ten, to catering in marquees for garden parties and weddings. It was all often on a knife edge, lots of smiles especially when the soup would spill and the pastries fall out of their packaging on route to the recipient! But that's showbiz!

We did reasonably well and used to tot up our rewards after checking on our outlay and use some of the proceeds for weekends away. It was one of these weekends when we drove our Vauxhall Viva to Llandudno to stay at the then Empire hotel, where I discovered the delights of Bloody Marys. Sliding off a barstool in my early 20s, dressed smart but not so used to intoxication - it was not such a pretty sight but I was in a state of exhaustion it could have been said. Dennis would assist me back to the room with a little effort and a smirk of mild embarrassment on his face.

Alex Munro Music Hall in Llandudno? Does anyone remember this end of pier show? A group of performers was not always a pretty sight on a windy wet night in Wales but the old pros they were had my admiration and respect. Not only did they perform, they sold the tickets, took you to the seats and sold the refreshments too. That's teamwork.

✱✱✱✱✱

Another episode that is lodged firmly in the brain is the time after we sold the house mentioned above to buy a glorified café we named the Bus Stop Grill. I realised after two months the smell of frying fat in my clothes and in the air was not for me! Dennis made this his full-time venture, whilst I continued as a charge nurse at the now defunct Rubery Hospital. He opened early and closed at 6pm. We did a good trade but profit margins were never huge. We also leased the building and did not own it so I soon realised I wasn't comfortable with this, never being fond of too many chips. Den as usual worked like a dog, organised and cleaned, cooked, built up the business. An all-day breakfast flew out the door and his cakes were gulped down with teas, coffees and fizzy drinks. A bevy of local businessmen, lorry drivers and workmen munched his food and kept us afloat, but I hated it. Decorated with black and white photos of the stars and showbiz people I knew it was more a reflection of my ego in its image than Dennis's. He just did all the hard work and I posed around like an old poof, helping myself to the till for the night out or a treat.

There was one occasion when there was a national bread strike and Dennis decided to flex his baking skills once more, as there seemed to be an untypical frenzy regarding bread supplies. As the baking stopped nationally, Dennis had lines of folk begging for more of his bloomers, and he was overwhelmed with the dependency of the British and their bread intake. The shop was full for his takeaway wholemeal and white-seeded breads all done in basic ovens, so much so that other customers could hardly get in to sit and eat their breakfast sandwiches and puds. He had started a bloomer avalanche!

After only one year I put the shop on the business market and luckily sold it and managed to make sufficient to buy a small, but beautifully-formed terrace in Florence Road, Acocks Green, Birmingham. We were to live the next 12 years in this place, a home of many tales and surprises and fun, heartache and joy. It was now 1975. Our first proper house was bought in 1972 and cost us £2,500. We saved a little and Dennis did extra work to save a decent deposit. To think you could spend that on a home entertainment system today or just a TV! Yes, economics, prices and costs were somewhat different then. Banks did not throw offers of mortgages at you based on income you didn't earn. We were pragmatic in those days and suspicious of easy credit. We paid for what we had.

Looking back as I tap this out, I realise that the 70s were more exciting than I ever thought at the time. We didn't seem too bogged down by so much political correctness and we were to have bin strikes, unrest and upheavals. So nothing changes does it? Only flared trousers have partly gone and don't seem to be too prominent now, and cars looked a bit desperate then, but fun on reflection.

Looking now over the room, my friend of 45 years, Viv, is reminding me of that era, and that as she lies on a couch covered in a snuggle rug she proclaims, "I saw two pregnant women today as I was driving through the village and it entered my head that when those children reach 21, if we make it we will both be 82." I just hope I get this all down before that age. It was still a few years to go before Margaret Thatcher became prime minister. I was yet to be 29 on her succession to that office in 1979 so logically in 1975 I was between mid 20 and death!

In 1975, I was busily making that terrace a little palace and a home inside. It was by those days opulent and comfy - small but different, with furniture in some rooms that were possibly too large, but plush to fall into. The nest and home making had always been part of me, making a place of safety and asylum from the traumas, self-made or otherwise of life.

On meeting Bill Buckley just a few years later, when he was a young reporter on the *'Sandwell Express and Star'*, which covers the whole of the Black Country conurbation, with a big circulation. He wrote a feature on me entitled "Bunny hopes to hop to stardom in fishnet tights". It was a large piece, well written and amusing and created interest from other journalists and radio stations, as my agent sent it around with other articles and information as a press release.

The black and white picture of me dressed as a demented rabbit was funny and different for the times and well before the famous Kenny Everett portrayal of "Cupid Stunt". The affectionate article covered my life and to date, sadly the article today is a little worse for wear and not up to standard to reproduce here.

I had some fun performing in that silly home-made outfit and it was a good way to raise a laugh and portray the trials of a camp, down-at- heel Bunny Boy competing in the glittering world of the Playboy Club in a sexually discriminating world loaded against men! As well as having to dress like that and serving in a fish and chip shop on the Edgware Road! I used to walk on the many stages and cabaret floors complete with a shopping bag and a cabbage in hand to mixed reactions and play off that image to good effect and stroke my bushy tail in my own inimitable way as described by one newspaper. My fishnets were black and thick with more ladders in them than a road map. Bill in this article said, "If Bunny is half as funny on stage as he is off he certainly will be a star." During these times I would mix the act with wearing a suit and also dress as a cleaner with full beard and moustache as well as occasional drag. Well it was all good fun and even now I occasionally resurrect it... usually when I am home and cooking a rabbit stew!

*****

Well in this decade, we didn't have mobile phones and many homes not even a landline, but I am reminded of the decade before and 1964. I was living in that small cramped, but clean home in West Bromwich and when Harold and Edith went out to the fantastically depressing pub directly opposite to this doll's house, my friend Viv and I set up grandiose evenings with table settings we never knew existed and prepared in suitable fashion on best china. Delights such as pickled onions, beetroot and any leftover salads added to by candlelight and low music. The table covering, I recall, was golden chenille.

Most conversations focused about laughing at our parents. Attitudes such as mine were much older and seemed more severe, laughing in particular at the thought of these oldies having sex which I knew they did, every Saturday night as a ritual despite their efforts to cover any noisy outbursts. I could hear the occasional grunt and noise and even I knew they didn't have a pig in that bedroom. It was declared at these dinners that we would be getting out of this area and possibly go abroad or move to a rural area or somewhere far more exotic and suited to our station in life. Sitting opposite each other in a world of our own thinking we were 'posh'. We both knew we were royalty and both had to get out of this place. We didn't know any other early teenagers who would want to do such things in our locality. Why did it all seem like summer? Perhaps it was.

It was this decade and I believed Viv was the only woman who could compete with Diana Rigg in *'The Avengers'*. She was my Emma Peel! We seemed to always fill our days and it never seemed like winter. I would go to Viv's parents and became an honorary family member or, as Viv's mum had five kids, I was the sixth poodle as she was to refer to her kids in later life. Viv and her husband have been in my life since before teenage years. The last decade for Viv, despite her tenacity, good works and dedication to all things, has seen her with the cruel diagnosis and accompanying horror of Trigeminal Neuralgia often known as the 'suicide pain'.

These sufferers can appear quite normal, then they will suddenly be struck down and overwhelmed with the most excruciating pain originating from the fifth cranial nerve. It's very hard to diagnose. Many unfortunates think it is to do with other dental-related problems and people desperately go and spend thousands of pounds, convinced its dentally related. There are not many specialists in this particular field. She had numerous investigations, I won't list them all. Suddenly, she decided to act on the advice of someone from the TN Association, an excellent support group for people with this disability. They put her in touch with the Walton Centre in Liverpool, one of only around 3 or 4 national centres. Evidence was found of some constitutional changes but treatments are limited to highly-toxic medications in her case.

Surgical procedures carry high risks and even freezing the nerve has its downsides so she manages this condition as best as the human spirit allows. I really try to be as supportive as I am able to be to her through these vile episodes, which are still frequent and debilitating. She remains to all who see her glamorous and fit. My God, she should have been a showgirl. We recently went to one of our jaunts to France to the peace and tranquillity of the Vendee but she was plagued with this foulness once more.

*****

CHAPTER 12

Jumping now to a momentous event in 2002, I met a guy (poor dear Dennis, I hear you cry). Dennis had started to go to bed extremely early, sometimes before even 9pm. I would have my evening partly alone when I wasn't doing the very odd show somewhere or singing for my supper. By 11pm or later I would sometimes go to a rather seedy haunt in the city.

On this particular evening (I used to stay around no more of an hour), I went genuinely to the loo, prior to going home. This very tall Asian guy with glasses and plainly dressed was washing his hands and was still washing them on my completion of ablutions. He looked, we smiled, then I was up against the wall in a most tender embrace and this in such a seedy dive. What could I do? (Slut!) I broke off this entanglement and pushed my one and only business card I just happened to have in my back pocket. Yes, my trousers were still up! I then fled in a state of ecstasy and dizziness to eventually fall asleep on my own in the house, as Dennis was snoring his tune and we had had separate sleeping rooms for our non-disturbed sleep for many years by now.

I attempted to put this incident in perspective but it was on my mind. I naturally told Dennis about it. He just smiled and we passed on to preparing dinner. While he did the cooking, I laid our old large refectory table.

Some three days later on a Sunday I answered the phone, well you do don't you? A quietly-spoken voice said, "Hello Thomas." It was the mystery man (I shall refer to him as 'A') and I told him that I was surprised at his call, stating that I didn't really expect to hear from him. We chatted extensively, doing the cat and mouse of discreetly negotiating around finding out a little more about each other. The conversation must have continued for the best part of an hour to Dennis's annoyance as Viv, her husband Gordon and her son Adam had called to visit and were sitting, chatting in the garden awaiting my return from this long phone conversation.

From that moment on I think I had a major personality change for the worse. I became besotted by him and it took up all my thinking and on meeting him I was convinced something special had happened (perhaps Dennis had seen it all before but I don't think like this). From a fairly in-control, decisive, independent, decision-making person I became like a dribbling fool and I didn't realise it. Was I going through a mid-life crisis? A bit late wasn't it?

As the days and weeks rolled on, I was to learn he was a practising doctor, a junior houseman at this time and working some 40 miles away. He would travel on most of his off duty to come to stay and be welcomed by both of us. I knew it was a hard, demanding life for a young man and made many allowances for that. The life of a doctor is one of constant training placements and progression into specialities and areas that are competitive and difficult to achieve. Many give up, some find a niche, while others plough through and hit their aims and succeed, to a point. Also, if you're not still the perceived ethnicity of choice and school tie, as well hidden as this may be, a lot of foreign doctors have it harder than most to prove their talents and skills. He was no exception, but very bright.

One weekend, he phoned to say that he was ill and had been in bed for almost five days with a fever and alone in a residence at his training hospital. I told Dennis, who insisted I go get him to bring him home to us and we would nurse him back to health with good cooking and pampering. As the weeks and months went by, it seemed to become a more semi-permanent arrangement. I was doing only occasional consulting work at this time and Dennis was taking on the role of Mother Earth. Dennis appeared, on the surface at least, to like him - no doubt thinking it's yet one more that will burn out. Little did I know. In fairness to A, he did say he had a commitment problem (who was I to talk, as along with me, came Dennis?). He also said he had problems with being faithful, but really wanted to try hard to be so. His sexuality generally outside the safety of the gay world was secreted away and not known to colleagues, family and friends. I did believe I could handle this.

I noticed his personality became more demanding, manipulative and good at winding me up. After staying a weekend, he would return to his new post in the north and leave me, stating, "I don't know when I'll see you, I may have things on." Yet having told me his on-duties and rotas I was always willing to drive to him. Dennis appeared to have no problem with this. Although bright and talented, A was provocative, bullying, dismissive and rude. I would, for some strange dependant unhealthy reason, put up with this and try to appease him to the point that I would be left frustrated and in tears. Why was I allowing this? (Maybe it was payback time you might think?) I had allowed him to control me for the first time in my life. Was I getting a taste of my own medicine? Arguments followed by intimacy. When he decided to be so.

Phone calls could be hard work with him and to get a straight answer to any question was dealt with short shrift. I was a mess. Dennis would see the state he would leave me in (yes I allowed it) and was in despair to see me so miserable, but I was blind to this personality trait and behaviour and would excuse it and tolerate it. My friends could see this unhealthy relationship but I wouldn't listen to any of their concerns. I was blinded by goodness knows what. A teenage love at 50! It was madness. His charm was only skin-deep and others caught him out too. He would taunt me and be amazing in front of others but occasionally it would crack and those experienced around me could see the flaws, the change in my behaviour and responses was very noticeable to them. I was in Danger Land. Within betrayal lies deceit. Some of the basic traits of human nature were to come home to roost.

*****

By around this time Dennis had a suspected embolism, but the pain he was experiencing to my mind did not concur with this diagnosis yet he was admitted to Solihull hospital for 'investigations'. I was not convinced - a series of bloods have to be routinely taken and screened. He often told me his pain was predominantly in his right side! Um, well tests had to be cancelled, as mayhem became standard in the ward, shutting down with outbreaks of infection. The usual bugs that are airborne in these mausoleums of misery. Well he was discharged, still unclear of the diagnosis but his pain noticeably worse. I arranged for him to be referred to a chest specialist. By the time his appointment arrived, the pain was excruciating. He had been receiving paracetamol, the magic analgesia for all ills. This now was my territory and I was going to advocate for him.

Dennis attended his locum consultant alone in the early stages. Now I was going everywhere with him to be with him and not as a passive observer. Letting the consultant rumble on, I sat patiently listening, digesting the information and the rhetoric.

Then I said my piece, "Doctor, I acknowledge your protocols and your clinical judgment but this man I have known for over 30 years, having lived with him all that time, and I am telling you he can not articulate his pain in words to you. This is why I am speaking up for him. He is not a malingerer; he is not a hypochondriac. He is in unmentionable, overwhelming pain. I know, I live with it every day. Even with this undiagnosed problem and we think we know what this will turn out to be, he requires palliative care immediately, not paracetamol! He can not wait for delayed test for days and weeks while he is in agony and without maximum pain relief NOW." I remained focused and polite but precise and made it clear that more robust and immediate treatment and particularly investigation needed to take immediate effect. He took his magic powerful pad and prescribed Oromorph. At last, something was happening - that was June or July of 2004.

No lung shadowing was showing nor any major deterioration when he had the bronchoscope, with me quietly present if you believe that. It was a mystery. He was weak and tired but still determined to fight. I sat each evening with him. We discussed his illness, we talked about all the things around – fears, life and not making it.

On knowing the definite diagnosis at last in the October of 2004, we set about talking about our life together, Dennis reinforcing that he wouldn't ever have changed a thing, me telling him how could I continue without him? Who would answer my bell when I rang it because no one would appear? How could I continue? How would I do it. Him facing it with a staunchness, but still intending to cling to every moment.

Of course, I was constantly telling him I was really tough and I would be practical and I would go on for him. I assured him that my cooking was up to his. We laughed a lot, but my face was always tear-stained and wet, especially when alone and out of his sight. I didn't really know what could ever be in front of me anymore, hoping we would have reached genuine old age like two crumbling old eccentrics together. It was not going to be. He pushed himself, but it was clear now the battle was lost. I would not leave his side and prepared the downstairs room, making it still a homely place. Whatever he wanted or needed I did it, except provide fags which, in his despair, even he grew tired of. The rest has been said - hearts were torn and broken. I threatened to have his ears removed and place them as a work of art on the fireplace, as I often made him smile with embarrassment when I went and rubbed those two large appendages on his lovely face and whispered silly nonsense to him. If he was soon to slip away from me I knew a part of me would be slipping away with him.

The realities we all have to face (the year before this Dennis did something else quite out of character). He had been drinking. I did not know that as I had never seen him drink in the late morning. He was jolly and I said that myself and A would return some DVDs I had borrowed from a friend. We were gone for around one and half hours. On our return there was no sign of Dennis. I found a note: "GOODBYE THOMAS."

I was shocked. We had rowed the previous day about his drinking, that I felt it was increasing, and he was becoming secretive and deceitful and telling me lies. I reported him missing. In my judgment, it was serious. The police went through their formality of checklists and kept me informed. I told them possible places he could have gone. My thoughts turned to Father Hudson's Home in Coleshill, the remains of the Father Hudson's Homes. Despite the horror of his stories, he was strangely attracted back on very rare occasions. That's what a blind faith does to the young - imprisons them, and I had gone with him twice whilst he met an ageing nun who he liked and was kind to him.

I was distraught; I was convinced he was dead somewhere. I started to mourn with anger and frustration, unable to sleep, pacing the house, phoning every lead I could connect to. He had never ever done this before. I pleaded with the police to find his body so I could at least know his fate, I was convinced he was not alive.

Five days passed with me in a demented state. A was quite cold and distant throughout saying, "Well he wouldn't last long with his health and after years of continual smoking." Thank you A. It was a lunchtime. The phone rang. It was a staff nurse at casualty department. Dennis had been found by some graveyard attendants, lying in a dugout grave, with what appeared to be a battered head.

We had a good friend living locally called Mike Parton who got on well with Dennis and had an affinity towards him, genuinely liking each other. Also, it was an opportunity to offload some of his disapprovals and frustrations about many things, as he was becoming unwell. Mike was a good comfort to him and besides, he needed a friend now other than just me. Mike would make himself available in any practical way he could, both when Dennis was well and unwell. Over a few years he gave much help; Mike Parton was a great comfort at a time of need. Well you can imagine, with that name he was obviously nicknamed Dolly!

Dennis was lucky. His exposure was extreme, his hypothermia ready to knock him off after almost five whole days in those exposed conditions. It was a miracle he was breathing. Just. Relieved, as well as pained, I was furious. I had been convinced that he was dead. I was in a state of high arousal and hurt. He told me a story that he had been attacked and robbed and fell after drinking half a bottle of spirit. Was this what his life had come to? Was I the cause of his mess? I was focusing on his needs. A was somewhat in the background, passing his snide comments and offering little support, yet telling me how grateful he was that we had all become his family and that he was part of it in every way. I was getting better by now at standing my ground - I knew where my loyalty lay.

That Christmas time, I took him with Viv and Gordon to our French house we had had since 1990, for Den to recuperate. A little hat on his head as thin as a bean, he bounced back a little but he was clearly not well, but as independent-minded as ever. By this time, he had himself admitted that he was drinking to excess and intended to sort out treatment, with me overlooking it. This was after I had dried him out over a weekend by mutual consent, using diazepam sleeping medication and watching out for the withdrawal symptoms. We got them as per all the theories and practice I have seen before a hundred times, so I knew what was to come.

He himself had decided on this more cold turkey approach. I would get to his GP after the weekend and get the Librium, together with the high doses of vitamin B to get him on the higher levels of prescribed medication to help him detoxify more safely. He was NOT going to any clinics. He was not allowed out of his room, which was stripped to a minimum as I, 'Nurse Ratchet', sat guard for three nights. I sat holding him as he hallucinated, shouting out, moaning and hitting out at whatever devils he could see. Drying out from alcohol is one of the worst things to watch, even worse than crack and heroin. It is legal and is the biggest misused drug in the world.

*****

During the better periods, Dennis decided that A should not have a bank loan or finance to buy a much-necessary car and that he would loan A the funds for a new vehicle. All of this led me to believe that Dennis did approve of this person within our life, as none of this influence came from me. A private pay-back, interest-free loan was arranged and over time it was all paid back. A was honourable in that way.

I began to notice my wine store was depleting as A would take a few for 'dinner parties' at friends whilst he was away from what he called his home here at Vernon Cottage. I would, on questioning him, be told of these many new friends but would never be invited or asked to any occasion with him. I was becoming suspicious. Eventually I was allowed into his private, growing new circle, under strict observation and by his choosing whom I would meet. Well, the few I met I really liked and we got on well. One particular couple being a French guy and his partner near to Sheffield.

By this time, Dennis was becoming noticeably more unwell. He would brush it off in his characteristic way of no fuss and getting on with it. I insisted we returned to his consultant again. X-rays, more tests, more investigation. Then alas, something strange was discovered after two months of eventually intense investigative explorations - a shadow, a large mass, suddenly appeared on the radar. Since July, nothing had been found. It was now October 2004. I told the consultant to phone me immediately anything was confirmed. He did. Dennis now had inoperable lung cancer, upper lobes affected. Four months to reach the inevitable diagnosis and now too late, apparently. I ran this by another doctor friend and he told me squamous cells have a way of being undetectable in the linings of the lungs for some time, and that standard X-rays don't always detect... until too late.

We spent many days slowly talking, discussing our lives, our past, our future again. Yes, he had one as far as we were both concerned. It was not curtains yet. We laughed so much in between the tears, mine often alone and out of his sight so as not to distress him more. He didn't break or crack; he was as pragmatic as usual. Still cooking, tidying the home as best he could, walking to the shops with the spirit of, "Must keep walking every day to the shops. Once I stop that it's curtains, have to keep the legs moving."

The weeks rolled on and he became weaker. The district nurses came in; they were amazing. All I could arrange was now in place. I was with him constantly. He was offered some respite at the local hospice. I wanted him home, but he jumped at it, demanding that I needed a rest! Typical! He spent a month there and I visited three times most days, then my father fell ill. I moved him into the previously-described field hospital of Flint Green Road. Amazingly, my neighbours years ago renamed it 'Freak Green Road'.

On the 7th January 2005, Dennis went into respiratory failure at home with me by the special bed, which was now in the former lounge. I got some medication into him and propped him up and assisted him in his breathing as best as I was able. I phoned 999, this was no time to arrange the hospice to take him; this was an emergency. Within minutes, the response was rapid. They incubated him, medicated him, relieving him of his distress and sped away, with me following the ambulance like some learner driver, speeding erratically in some 1950s American 'B' movie.

I stayed by his bedside in intensive care, relieved for his temporary respite and assured that he was now being managed for this emergency, but not for long. Just prior to this, my father was admitted to the same hospital, so after Dennis was settled (conscious but unable to communicate in words) I went to see Harold, who even in his own exhaustion knew all was not well. I explained briefly that Dennis was in another ward and kept it short. Harold looked on in melancholy with his dogged face and sad eyes, head bowed and frowned. No words needed to be exchanged. I returned to Intensive Care, satisfied myself Dennis was stable, saying I would let him rest and return. A had been informed and was insistent he would come home, how very kind of him!

I flew back home to prepare once more to return to the hospital a few hours later. I quickly showered. A arrived and I filled him in with some of the happenings. He looked concerned and was quiet. The phone rang. It was the French man, who I shall call John. For 30 minutes, he unravelled a story regarding his partner's recent suicide attempt, his profound depression and his dealing with him at home.

A had some months earlier asked me to entertain them both to see if I could assist the partner with some professional help and convince him to seek some therapy. He was telling John that it was related to stress at his work place. I did undertake this weekend of therapy and he agreed to seek some help. I was never convinced of his underlying explanations and rationalisations; I knew something was up. Then the bomb dropped. John had constantly pushed at his partner to open up for months. Now I was to be told the cause of his behaviour. He had been seeing A and was inconsolably in love with him, even after being told after many encounters it could come to nothing. He, like me, had become 'besotted' to the point that now, even A was now getting anxious, as he couldn't manipulate himself out of this situation and might get caught out. He was turning up at A's workplace, begging and breaking down. That would never do would it? For a doctor no less. He had been turning up and waiting near the car park where A left his car.

I was asked if I would tell A not to visit them any more, as by now John was on guard and preventing yet another suicide attempt and was beside himself. Well we all know the dangers of playing with fire don't we, and A was more than capable of lighting quite a few. John said he wished to sever contact with him. A was aware I was on the phone and I used my skills to cover the fact that this conversation had happened by telling him that John was enquiring regarding Dennis. I suddenly became calm. Truth is stranger than fiction. As I replaced the receiver the phone rang once more, "Mr Bunn?"

"Yes." I replied.

"I am so sorry to inform you that Dennis has passed away."

What timing. No dramatist could have written it. I managed to say I would be right there and I asked the question around the circumstances, as he had been stable when I had left some two hours ago. The nurse told me that, on being 'transferred' to another ward, he had died and was dead on arrival. There. So much for intensive care. My thoughts were cynical as ever, the staff knowing he was terminally ill and that life-saving bed was required for someone who may make the longer term. The practical brain kicks in. I told A I was off to the hospital alone to see Dennis now, dead in a single lone room.

As most people who experience this, my thoughts were the ones of guilt and confusion for not being there at the exact moment of his demise. As I saw it, he was alone with medics, strangers and not me at the moment of final departure. It's a normal reaction. One you relive and invent throughout your life to nurture the person and to continually want to make a better ending for yourself. Perhaps I could have made them keep him in Intensive Care for longer, he may have had a little while longer with me. All those things go through the traumatised thoughts. Recounting, rechecking your own input to a situation and asking yourself - could you have done anything better?

*****

Besides, the other distraction was my dealings with A who had become quiet and thoughtful, no doubt in anticipation of my unknown reaction to the death of Dennis. Little did he know. As we know, we go into automatic coping mode. I returned to see Dennis. He had been placed in a small room. Lying in this state of grace alone didn't seem very graceful to me.

His physicality gone, motionless, lifeless, never to wake again. He had not been certified officially dead. A nonsense, I have always thought. Absurd having to be the province of a medic, but then they do need to eventually sign the death certificate so that you drag yourself back to the place of death to collect it. He was dead, I could tell. I know about such things because I was a nurse! Eventually some young man arrived who had never met him, as is usual, and he confirmed the status.

I sat quietly with Dennis for the last time and had the one-sided conversation I had often had with him when he had been living. Tear-stained and quiet, I sat for what seemed an age. I don't recall how long, but no one came to kick me out or offer a cuppa, but then what do you expect? They are institutions of misery, joy, hope and fear. I said my goodbyes and slowly drove, eyes streaming like it was rain on the windscreen. Returning to the house and A for yet another unwritten episode to come.

The theory of bereavement reactions is generally true. Irrespective of the inevitabilities of the death. There is still shock and disbelief and the instant activity of organisation, then idealisation of the lost person kicks in. I was no exception to this rule, yet I had another separate task in hand.

I kept my mouth closed for once and said nothing of the conversation of the earlier phone call from John and contained myself, not an easy skill for me. My mind was on other things. I would save this one for later. A looked worried and was being quietly supportive, or embarrassed, but there was no conversation coming from me, which he must have picked up from my nonverbal communication. Stillness and peace seemed to transfix me as I felt amazingly strong as to what I was about to undertake.

I told A that I didn't intend to cook and that we would go out to dinner. We both quietly prepared. As we clambered into my car and drove away, I spoke in a very measured manner. After about five minutes and well on the way to the eatery I proceeded with, "The phone call I received from John was enlightening. He was telling me in great detail of his partner's deep depression and the problems he has had to deal with over the last few months. It was quite a worry but as John said he eventual broke down and told him every detail after hiding it for so long. Obviously, the recent overdose was a trauma for all, and YOUR affair with him was the cause of it. Seems you got out of your depth this time A and couldn't control that one could you? You really need more experience than you have, both of mental health, fragility of others and disordered personality. You need to look at yours, you fucking bastard."

He was now thinking on his feet. Or the car seat this time, I was in control.

"Well I have more important matters in hand, I will deal with you later."

Have you ever seen a south Indian blush? He did a lot of it. His circulation was well speeded up. In my head this relationship was over but I was not about to kill it. He more than likely wanted free of it any way. I had just lost the most important one to a dreadful disease and I needed to think through and deal with my reactions over the coming hours and days. As I often said, we are all victims of our own disordered personalities. My manifestation was quite different than A's in that I may have been devious in my past at times, but most of my life had been lived out openly and as honestly as I know, having the many flaws for all to see, but I always strived for openness.

This liar sitting next to me was babbling excuses now as to why he couldn't end his northern experience. He actually admitted to it, said he was out of his depth in managing this affair; that the guy who by now was in a dreadful shape. When he was told that A wanted no more to do with him, the outcome was not to be smooth. It wasn't going to be so easy to dump this one was it? I was much later to discover the pattern to this behaviour of the wise and wonderful A. Do I sound bitter and twisted by any chance? The dangerous games that some people play.

We arrived at the restaurant, went inside and took our table. I was firm-faced, matter of fact. I was enjoying seeing him squirm, as it had never happened before. There are so many different ways to punish and I have been around long enough to know. Doctor or no doctor, I had seen how childish and stupid he could be, as well as his displays of arrogance that he had in abundance. A characteristic he was to openly deplore in others. I was strong again. Thank you Dennis. I did feel he was guiding me through this and there was more to come - I hadn't finished yet.

There had been so many incidents of his foulness in the recent past, too many to mention. Due to my unhealthy dependence I just let myself submerge into a drivelling wreckage but now I was back on form, doing it my way. Had Dennis rejuvenated my sparkle perhaps? I could see fear in his eyes for the first time, not for any other reason, I suspect at this stage, other than he had been found out. But he could see I had changed in this moment of crisis, perhaps he was pleased and looking for a way out. The warning shots had been firmly blasted over his head. Maybe this was a coward's way out too. Anyway, I maintained what was left of my dignity and self-control (I had not had much of it in the last three years) and Dennis had to witness this in his desperate hours.

On arrival home I settled in with A. He was in a quiet state of apprehension but he didn't just walk out and go, which could have been one option for him. In his own way he had invested a lot in his relationship with me no matter how I tell it here. No matter how warped and dysfunctional it was. It may be by his standards the nearest to a commitment. Something I knew he never really could manage in any relationship.

Whilst he was upstairs in the top attic bedroom I lectured him on personality disorder saying, horribly, had he heard of Harold Shipman? I continued on to describe the 40-plus different categories in the classification of diseases and, with no rehearsal I continued my offensive. I became eloquent-positive in control, a real bitch. Perhaps Bette Davis had entered me. I pointed out his personality traits and told him that most surgeons must be warped to want to slice people open. The macabre nature of it excused only by the social good we subscribe to it. That he was cold, distant and incapable of warm real attachments. That's why he chose to be a butcher! Sadistic and monstrous were some of the endearing points I made regarding his behaviour over the last three years. Telling him his personality was not commensurate with his profession in butchery. And that he should change his speciality (he did eventually).

I lectured him on the inability to learn from experience, reverting to type and that his charm was, as like all psychopaths, superficial and thrill seeking (I should know). He was a menace to society and people at large I bellowed, but told him that his bedside manner was good simply because he only had to stay at any bedside for around five minutes. Even he could sustain that! He couldn't and didn't utter a word as I told him I would probably keep this tirade up for hours and just break off for a drink and return. I did! And he tolerated it.

Three years of enforced repression, I was madder than any cat let out of a bag. After around an hour of manic vitriol, where I got the energy from I'll never know if I live to be 99! Instantly I decided on one more tactic. I walked to him and slapped him right across his face. Assault, I hear you cry! Totally inappropriate. You better believe it! The force of my blow knocked him to the other side of the room. He staggered to his feet and I repeated it. With the message, "Just so you remember my words." He could have struck back. He was tall and strong in stature and in every way looking a tough specimen of manhood. He didn't defend himself at all, saying he deserved it. Was this truth at last?

I never advocate violence in any relationship, so children at home and social workers and non-poofs please read this. DON'T DO AS I DID! Well perhaps in exceptional circumstances. Besides I had just lost Dennis forever. Exceptional methinks, and timing was not so good.

I had learned that he had had a series of elder gentleman that always seemed to end a little strangely but soon after the break-up he managed to 'stay friends with them'. They all appeared comfortably off and many had good social circles and would all include A. He loved my friends too, as they were such a large diverse crowd. I did not intend being put onto some fallback list of past encounters. He was quite able to manipulate suitable arrangements with this group of past encounters, for a drop in, or a meal out, a night out or a weekend away. Was I that daft, as innocent or complicit as it may or may not have been? No way was I having him floating in and out of my life on his whim. It needed to be tidied up, but all in good time.

Over those next few weeks he came and went. I behaved as though things were healing and was getting to a manageable point. At least I wasn't using slap therapy now. There were a few incidents yet to occur, and secretive behaviours I had come to expect. I was not too pleased when he told me he had left his sister's place where he was supposed to be studying whilst he was working for his ongoing exams and moved in with another old friend and former shag. But why should I bother? So I played the game. I said, "Good, I'll come up and stay." That threw him off balance.

He had moved from his sister's place and was now staying at this other guy's place as it was more convenient. Then they went out to dinner. Because of accommodation 'difficulties' A arranged for me to stay with another 'old friend' of his and left me in his hands. Whatever plans I may have imposed on him, I took some amusement from it, still angry that this dinner date did not include me!

I phoned A and his companion whilst deep in the middle of their meal, discussing whatever. No, I didn't phone A, I phoned his dining companion whose number I already had and proceeded to tell him I was also in

London and had not been invited to join them for the meal. This dinner date of A immediately invited me over. I thanked him but declined the offer. Besides, look at all that support A was giving me. He worked on a need-to-know basis and did not like people knowing anything about his movements. Perhaps he had another life as a secret agent!

*****

Months earlier, some friends were throwing a garden party. I was the turn. Viv's brother and his wife put this event on. A came and was sociable and enjoying it as far as I could determine. Suddenly, Helen the host, who knew A engaged with him and told him of another doctor who she was working with. He must know him and his name was '?' She continued to make the links. He became stony silenced, stony-faced and walked off. He didn't want anyone making connections like that. His response to that interaction rang many bells. He didn't make contact with Helen again. What on earth could we possibly put together from such reactions? Secrets and lies. They always get caught out. If you have no secrets and are honest it's a less dangerous game, even if people don't like you for it.

You are true to who you are. Well, like all of us he was influenced by his culture, the need to survive. But I have never yet seen many of these doctors from some deprived continents return to develop their own infrastructure and commit their lives to improving the lot of the ordinary folk, seeming happy to get up the ladder and obtain some status. Is there really a genuine concern for their own countrymen, seeing understandably a more comfortable life here? The Tsunami bought that home to me. He had the opportunity to return to his homeland when they seemed desperate for doctors to assist in the provision of health care for the traumatised and injured. Every excuse was made not to return and he justified that one very well indeed.

I managed some degree of containment till then, as I wanted to lull him into a false sense of security. He still had given no real indication of wanting out. Then I pounced. A phone called again from London to say he couldn't come on the date that he had arranged to return. I now informed him of my own arrangements. By now he had accumulated quite a lot of stuff at the house. It was going to be an easy task. I told him

I wanted him out of my house by a given date and if he didn't arrange to get his good friend to collect all his belongings, I would drive to his hospital and dump them in reception at outpatients where his close friend, a young doctor herself, worked. She was the one person he did ditch his shit on.

I believed that she too loved him in her own needy way, but maybe she was bright enough to know what she would be in for, having witnessed his previous history. A knew I meant it. His time had come. I think he was always expecting this or doing what people do, setting up his exit strategy. Perhaps, as said before, he thought, "Well you ended it, so I don't have to."

I spent the next week packing his substantial belongings. Books galore, clothes in abundance - so much stuff but I packed it reasonably well. My urge was to throw the lot onto the lawn in the rain but I never liked an untidy garden. Besides, it wouldn't land on his head. He now had his deadline fast approaching and his friend, a charming young doctor in medicine, came, distraught at the manner of the ending. She was not so surprised as she had witnessed endings before it seemed. Those were more manageable perhaps and parted on reasonable terms with some. He really knew how to get them, but getting rid of this one was not so easy.

Naturally, not all of his belongings could be taken but some things could be taken in one fell swoop. His messenger and pick-up service would return by mutual agreement. Some I decided to keep as compensation for distress, free board and lodgings, financial assistance and for stress-induced madness. I didn't return some items and had no compulsion in not doing so. Some we had purchased separately, some jointly. So at least he's always remembered.

I think that is why still, some six years later, he attempts communications with me. However, it is common behaviour for the disordered personality to lull you into a false sense of security and try tactics again when it seems a safe time lapse. They get older; they get more desperate. When the charms don't work so well. Some become potentially dangerous as their attractiveness looses its appeal. Look out you older fools!

One good point regarding him. I believed he genuinely saw Dennis and I as a family who had taken him in at a raw time of his life, who cared about him and we truly did. I still believe he may miss some of those times - some of them good. He had a feeling of a sort of family away from the lie he had lived in his own socially-structured society. He was comfortable with himself. He will survive well. He will be playing his game as we all do, as insights and behaviours are difficult to alter deeply. Yet there is always emotional cost somewhere. That's life if you engage in it.

He did once tell me that in Buddhism you are reincarnated as another being or animal and return until you get life right. He did say he would return as a 'snake' so at least he must have had some insight. Perhaps he was expecting to build some life with me after Dennis - I don't really know. I would never have wanted this, it's now time to be alone and not some dependent mess hanging onto a fantasy. Get a grip at my age for goodness.

I did not let him enter the house again, apart from once in a mellow phase where he reinforced those things about me and Dennis, really making him his family and all that stuff. He told me on that occasion to keep the things I had not returned as he had nowhere to put them and the rightful place was my in my house. I duly obliged. So when he phoned over a year later to ask if he could possibly have them I answered an affirmative, "No." I suggested he sue me and I had the hat and pearls ready and fixed for the judge! They say time heals. Are we really so sure?

As I mentioned, if I could practice the philosophy of the Buddhist it would be a great salvation for anyone, as that system of belief is borne not out of a god but the frailties of mankind. It is more a science of the mind as Buddha was a human being, not a god and what was offered by him was an experience of living and his teachings were experiential. This philosophy has affected my inner self greatly. You can see why it sleeps easily by the side of a more therapeutic approach in psychiatry.

At the core of his teachings is that we suffer and are carried away with emotions and thoughts that are both positive and negative and that we are also boundless containers, sharing the same nature as all other beings. Cravings and attachments bring both of these positive and negative experiences to us. The main difference from other ideologies is that it is non-sectarian, non-judgemental, unconcerned with dogma, race disability or sexuality. It urges with us to be compassionate with ourselves as well as others. It's a practical vision of life that asks us to live in the here and now, yet encourages meditation and mindfulness.

As for sexual misconduct, Buddhism makes no distinction between straight and gay sex, or other expressions of sexuality. Sex is the focus and is viewed as similar to many other human functions like anger, hunger, joy and fear as well as happiness. In fact, to feel all these emotions, both positive and negative, is the very essence of being alive. Interestingly, a Buddhist monk and writer did describe sex as '...a porcupine going into a rat hole - easy to go in, yet very difficult to come out.' Within Buddhism you will find talk and discussion about sexual activity when it causes harm to yourself or others and that gay sex is not ever seen as sexual misconduct when it is between two consenting adults. If it is not resulting in harming others, all sex has the same status. It is the impact that may be of concern.

For instance, if sex is being had with others outside an attachment of a life partner where commitment has been made. If what takes place in the full knowledge of the other and has their approval, it is not seen as evil or bad. Die-hard traditionalists will no doubt never accept this. In fact, my journey through life has revealed the damage that orthodox religions have done to the vulnerable and not so strong in our society, or where parenting has been so indoctrinated with religion that it has been a major contributing factor to mental ill health.

The above also applies to straight married couples too. Sex is just sex, no more, no less. All of us have to judge the situations we may find ourselves in mindfully. This belief would also stress that strong desires and attachments can make us act 'unmindfully' and cause harm to others and to ourselves as in contracting or passing on any sexually-transmitted diseases, so we need to be mindful and aware of our situation when embarking on our quest for pleasure and joy. Ultimately, there is no evil in attaining deep fulfilment and becoming fully awake as a human being.

Much is written regarding Buddhism from a western perspective. I only know what I know and take from it what I see as positive in my life. You will make up your own minds for sure. The nearest section of similar beliefs in a western sense, if you study its true relevance, is Quakerism. Less of a religion as such and more a reflective state of being. A very accepting movement and useful to know about in any search for some sense of self in this world of others. I know my two friends, Chris and Clive, have an interest in its influence on the self. Yet feel no compulsion to join in any formal sense, as there is no pressure to do so, as there is in some rancid evangelical institutions of traditional religion.

Let's move on. Let's see what pours. Returning to the aftermath of the relationship with A.

*****

CHAPTER 13

Cars have played a part in all our lives and in order to undertake the work I did, both as an NHS employee and an entertainer, as soon as I was in a position to have them, I did - they were a necessity if ever you need to get to any destination on time. Even before I could afford them I bought old cars from the age of 17, having passed my test, as soon as I was allowed, at the huge cost of one pound, two shillings and sixpence!

The first one was a derelict Jag Mark 9. I couldn't drive that as I purchased it before 17 and therefore Gordon would drive us around in it and demonstrate its power. It was cheap and had been traded in for a sparkly new one, so I got a bargain - well not in petrol terms. I recall then a Ford Popular that had three forward gears and was blue.

The first one I really loved was bought with Dennis in late 1969 and was an MG 1100 with a lovely walnut dashboard, in British racing green. I loved that car. Until one day, driving from the hospital with Ken, my friend from Highcroft, I was to break suddenly for prevention of a collision to find the bottle of milk I had bought with other stuff plonked on the back seat smashing forcibly into the car, smashing into pieces. Have you ever tried cleaning glass and milk up in a car? Well for months and months afterwards, the smell of gone-off milk lingered in the nostrils.

I had a series of Citroens for economy reasons including the eccentric 2CVs; a grand old Rover 100 was a joy until one night I parked it outside on a main road whilst doing a gig in the city centre, as it had not got any restrictions at night. The fog came down and I was informed that a bus had ploughed into the rear of it, so I drove around with that for a while as it was stainless steel boot and not easy to fix. I believe the bus didn't look too grand either.

Many others passed through my fingers, like a lovely late-1960s Wolseley and motors like that. There was also a Spitfire sports car that spent more time off the road than I spent on it. My Mercedes 3000 was a beauty and good for posing, but the most reliable was a great 90s Volvo, the most reliable despite being told that it was an old man's car.

The one I purchased as a bit of showbiz was a beautiful, beige Jaguar mark VII 1957 model with a split-window screen. On selling it, I gave profits to a children's charity, giving me a bit of publicity in the papers and in the Midlands with me posing over the bonnet like an idiot in jeans and boots and mohair jumper. Michael used to love to drive me to a gig, or through the street, or as a pick up from an airport in chauffeur's hat and blazer. He was a real actor when it came to that lovely old classic. I sold it eventually and it was driven all the way back to Munich by an eager German man. I wonder if he still has it. Well, cars are cars and not to be possessive over people is what counts, so back to this decade and continuing with post Dennis's death. And the ending I talked of before with A.

*****

Some months went by and as often in our lives, Robert, my old friend I told you about earlier who I used slap therapy on in those late 60s, decided that we should get together to undertake a ritual to rid ourselves of our evil and insane feelings and to purge ourselves. Robert would provide garlic and lemons, I would provide the knives and direct the free-floating chanting. I decided the place for the ritual ceremony would be the kitchen and that we would chant completely naked! Like some old ancient cult.

Robert himself had just gotten rid of someone after a decade of determination, never to enter those emotional depths again. So this was a dual ritual to rid ourselves of both our own madness and, as we saw it, the evilness of others in our lives. Perhaps we are just a pair of old inadequate individuals propping ourselves up with theatricality, but it seemed very therapeutic and necessary at this time. We just went with the moment and bawled out our madness - it spilled and flowed. We entered into it most vigorously and ended up speaking in loud tongues, more Swahili-like than anything European, scattered with a few choice expletives. I recommend it to anyone – it's cheaper than paying for private therapy and the NHS doesn't indulge so much in Gestalt these days. Well in truth, Gestalt therapy concentrates on what is happening right now rather than what is being talked about - in that sense, it is seen as an existential theory. I am all for here and now as that is all there is.

Talking of 'madness', I am reminded of my first meeting with a patient at the old Central Hospital in Hatton, Warwick. It was at the beginning of my tenure there in 1980. I was a Clinical Tutor and on my second day of being in the School of Nursing I decided to venture out and wander around the wards and introduce myself to staff and patients whom I did not know. As I was about to enter the main grand door of this gothic pile on a sunny day I was met by a woman who I will refer to as May. She had hand on hip, smoking a fag, looking dishevelled and staring me in the face. I got in first and said, "I am Tom and I work over there and who are you then?"

"You're a bit of all right love. What you doing here then? I am up on Woodville with sister. Have you got a fag love?"

"I don't smoke May", I replied.

"I'VE JUST BEEN ****D BY A DONKEY LOVE, OVER THERE", bellowed May.

I proceeded to find the ward that May had hailed from, as I wanted to see the place in which she resided and the other delightful people it contained and cared for. These ladies were a constant challenge to the ward staff and the sister Mary Wesson. She was a good woman who understood her charges better than anyone and often spoiled and protected them although in full blue uniform before the pressures of civvies were put upon her. I watched her interactions with her patients and she was amazing, never harsh never cruel, always fair and long-suffering and willing to be available at any time. She had the respect of her charges and me, as many were grossly thought-disordered and quite long-stay, by then what would be called continuing care. This ward was full of the most intriguing and difficult personalities. I was to get to know many of them and all their idiosyncrasies over the next few years and they were unwittingly to feature in many of my illustrative lessons for students in the field of psychiatry.

I used to not only observe those odd schizophrenic behaviours - I would absorb them. Not unhealthily into myself and I would often portray these oddities in my own mannerisms with Dennis and friends. They often had to endure my portrayals of pseudo-madness when they were in my company, and I could keep it up for hours, those poor souls.

One lady, I'll call her Madge, used to fly into this ward I told you about and have a tea towel draped over her shoulders and shout a tirade of completely bizarre thoughts. All excited, she would bellow, "I have just flown in from Russia and I must go back in a minute." Jumping and jerking, she was manic and gregarious and sang and danced around when she was high on her fantasies and expressed her joy. All this while the staff would persuade her to take a break from her imaginary flights and eat her lunch.

Then there was Miss Jones, as she had to be called. She would slowly walk by with her handbag, hair pinned in a severe bun, muttering obscenities under her breath, looking disdainfully at anyone who dared ask or question her. She was, after all, Queen Victoria and no rational confrontation to any delusional belief would or could ever diminish such belief. Even being on a ward in a psychiatric hospital and having her own room that was filthy and full with dirty clothes would not change this fixed belief - it was classic.

When she had left the ward, which she would attempt to do most mealtimes, not because the food was bad but because she couldn't sit with others who were beneath her. The battles 'royale' that we had persuading her to bathe were the dilemmas facing the nursing staff, as the lives lived in delusion are not compatible with day-to-day functioning and self care as you and I might know it. Each Thursday, at around 11am, Miss Jones would, handbag at the ready, quietly walk down to the hospital reception and sit waiting for her Daimler car to pick her up to transport her to Barclays bank. When on being asked why, she would quietly utter, "To get the salaries for my staff."

Needless to say, a Daimler never arrived but she would sit there for hours, refusing to depart until it arrived. Reports would be filtered back via Cyril on the switchboard as to her disposition. At regular intervals she would, after a few hours of interspersed contact with 'her staff', return to the ward to partake of refreshment, always uttering posh obscenities under her breath. In reality, in her younger life, she had been in service and shared a little terraced house with her sister. A far cry from her majestic beliefs.

The flying lady that I call Madge, a few months later, took to deciding to eat her own waste product! Her answer being, "Well it's my shit, I'll eat it if I want to!" This phase did pass when I suggested another psychiatrist who she adored be asked to have a word with her, as for some unknown reason he had a good relationship with her though he hardly knew her. She was asked to sit awhile and use his skills to dissuade her from this latest disgusting craze. After smiling sweetly into his face she told him, "Don't be silly and fuck off." But from that day onwards she stopped this unhealthy diet!

Some of these symptoms are not seen quite so florid these days for many reasons of better management and different regimes, but they do still exist and are alive and well, hiding behind the community doors of openness and tolerance, or in some cases misunderstanding and neglect. When the delusions are not of a harmful or persecutory nature these behaviours give little threat to others but first they need to be spotted, diagnosed, understood and managed. It is normal that these persons will never in the early stages comply with treatment, so it's important than when and if it becomes threatening to themselves or others it is acted upon. Sadly, this doesn't always occur. It's still possible for people to slip through that community net and the psychiatric services who are overstretched and burdened can themselves fall victim to terrible outcomes.

It's never so newsworthy to lead a newspaper story with the successes of the community care approach as those folk go relatively unnoticed and fit in well. Besides, what editor would want a story of 12 mentally ill people who settled into community life over the last ten years, being successfully managed and are leading relatively normal lives? No doubt you will think my earlier ranting with Robert and our purging ceremony was as bizarre and as crazy as my former charges but at least we convinced ourselves that we have insight!

*****

At this moment I have flown to Thailand again in September 2010 and been making my jottings and wondering and reflecting on this exercise. My main thought being that Dennis, I believe, would have loved the hustle and bustle, and the ability to seek somewhere calm and quiet at the same time. It is on these occasions that I miss him more but I am lucky to be able to travel with an old friend, Roger, who is as barmy as me and as difficult! This is what he has kindly written about me:

> Well I suppose it was around the mid-70s when I met Thomas Bunn, who I shall now affectionately call Bunny. I was invited by a friend to a dinner party where Bunny and his partner Dennis were also invited. We soon got into conversation and found out that we had the wonderful Dorothy Squires in common. Bunny invited me to his home to talk about her and show me some photos he had of Dorothy.
>
> I called around one evening and rang the bell. The door opened a little way and there stood a young man, naked! I was taken aback and asked, 'Does Thomas live here?' Before the young man could answer, Thomas had yelled from upstairs, 'Come in love, take a seat, down in a minute!' Well, yes he was soon down in dressing gown, as he is mostly these days too, as he asked the young man now in a dressing gown to make, '...two coffees love.'
>
> Well I stayed a few minutes and left, as at this time I felt a little uncomfortable. I saw the photos and left, but from this meeting we were to become friends for what is now a long time ago.
>
> We visited Dorothy's concerts together in Wales at the famous White Wheat Club in Maesteg where Dorothy gave a good concert and we were able to say, 'Hi' to Jenny Pitman. who was the first lady trainer to win the Grand National. She was training Dororthy's horses at the time, including Esban who went on to win the Scottish Grand National.
>
> Another visit was to see Dorothy in Cabaret at the Hollywood Inn at Gorseinon. This was hardly Hollywood though, up a one-track road, but again Dorothy came up with a good evening of song. Afterwards, stopping her car to say hi to us, especially to Bunny who she had known many years.

We often had visits abroad to Amsterdam and Paris and also stayed in Rotterdam with a couple of Bunny's friends. Over the years we have sometimes not been in touch for months, but when we were in contact with each other it was as if we had never been apart - the sign, I feel, of a lasting friendship.

After the sad loss of Dennis and the loss of a very close relative of mine, we seem to have come together on a more permanent basis. We speak or are in contact most days and have recently taken to long holidays together in Thailand, a place Bunny told me I would love years ago, but until last year I had never ventured there.

The place we go to is Phuket - we are quite well known there now. One evening, Bunny took me to a go-go bar where the boys dance with only a skimpy pair of underpants. The place was busy and sat next to us was a Japanese man who was, to say the least, a little drunk. He had a boy on his lap, and the stage in this seedy place was full of nearly-naked boys. All of a sudden, the Japanese customer fell to the floor, nearly knocking Bunny's drink with him. Bunny jumped up, looked around and exclaimed, 'Well what a state to get yourself into in a place like this.' We looked at each other and all that was going on around us and I said, 'Well love, it's hardly the Ritz.' To which we fell about laughing and had to leave, helpless with laughter.

We often have such fun on these holidays such that, as we say, they have become legendary.

Some years ago, Bunny introduced me to another theatrical friend whom I often took to concerts and looked after. One weekend before Christmas, some years ago, I went with her to the then Whiteleys Shopping Centre where she wished to buy a Scalextric set for her grandson, which she did. She wore a large overcoat with large sleeves. When we arrived back home she was in fits of laughter. 'What's the matter?' I said. She said, 'Well they charged me for the set but I got away with this', to which she produced from her coat sleeves, several cars and other items to accompany the set she had bought for her grandson. It was just like a Margaret Rutherford scene in one of her old movies. I was so surprised at all this - thank God there was no electronic tagging in them days.

So there is so much more to say of Bunny and my friendship, but that's it for now. Bunny has been my friend, as I said earlier, for well over 30 years and it's not over yet, with more holidays planned and much more besides.

In the words of Dorothy, 'Is That All There Is?' Oh no, he is not ready for that final curtain yet and when he is, I know like us all, he will be saying, 'Is that all there is to dying?'

*****

After a slow walk in the town of Patong in Phuket, then a dash into an air-conditioned mall called Jungceylon, I begin to think I must return to the hotel room to continue inflicting these pages both on you and myself. As I am prostrate on the bed, my mind wanders to Dennis once more and his relationships with our neighbours in Acocks Green. He was far more laid back than me, but the friends we made in that road would have their own tales to tell of him.

A couple of years before his death he took to doing a few unsolicited jobs for them, like cutting the lawn for one of them, and doing some tidying in another garden as he said he wanted to keep busy and help a little. One weekend I decided to go away to mid Wales to see my two friends Chris and Clive, as we had toyed with the idea of living there and we thought Viv and I would survey the place and look at property prices. Little did I know then that all that would be put on hold as Dennis would never make it. It was some two years after his demise that I did move there myself alone.

On settling down for a drink, the phone rang. It was Dennis calmly chatting to Chris. He was passed to me and he said, "I've had a little accident. I have cut the top of my finger off!"

"What?" I replied, "How the hell did you do that?"

"Well I was mowing the lawn and the mower stalled so I checked it out and… need I say more?"

Instead of sympathy I barked, "For goodness sake, don't cut the hedges with the electric cutters. You will sever your bloody head off!"

He was becoming accident prone. Little did I realise he was increasing his alcohol consumption and not always reserving it for his usual night-time drink. It was during this phase I was to discover his many mishaps. Like for instance when our next door-but-one neighbour, Karen, went away for a break. Dennis decided to tidy up her front path and garden that had been a little neglected due to her busy working life. Only he didn't stop at the tidying part. He decided to paint all her rockery and place it in a neat edging pattern up the path. He painted the stones royal blue!

I couldn't believe it when I saw it. I asked him, "Did you ask her before you embarked on this?"

Dennis stated he had been given a free reign to do what he thought best. However, I wasn't convinced that his choice was in the best interests of his new-found altruistic endeavours. Karen, realising Dennis meant well, pretended she liked it as she had gathered he was far from well and those stones were left in site until after his death. Thank you Karen.

*****

Of all the places in my life I have visited, I often went alone, due to Dennis's working schedules. Canada, Australia, West Africa, Malta, the Balkan states, USA, Poland, most of Europe and beyond. Those times he did join me were happy and memorable. He loved India and loved the relaxed pace of the south. He always said he could see himself living amidst it all - a dream I was happy to indulge in. He seemed at peace there and loved the food and the pace of it, as long as he could consume oodles of strong coffee and his cigarettes.

However, the house we had purchased in 1990 in the Vendee region of France was to prove he had a more on-off relationship with that place. It was purchased on a whim for my 40th birthday - well that was my rationale for it. I informed Dennis over the phone what I had done, telling him he would love it. For a while he did.

I had ventured to this region with a work colleague, Rene Mathieu, who was at that time Director of Nursing. She herself was French, but spoke with a slight Coventry accent. She had gone to seek out a house in that region and decided to purchase quite a large project in the village of Bazoges En Parades. She had had her children, now all grown up, and felt it would be big enough to accommodate them all at holiday times and, should they all overlap or visit together, then a larger place like this would be ideal.

Journeying around with her and a trusted agent, we saw many properties before she settled on the one mentioned and as we viewed properties, I became consumed with the idea that I also should invest in a holiday retreat for Dennis and myself. I saw something I liked, in need of some general love and care but solid and reasonable with barns attached and secluded in a small hamlet, near enough to a town for major provisions. It was unspoilt, and still is to some extent today, though it has all been partly gentrified to some degree, but not to the point of destruction of its original identity.

In the 21-plus years that I have held on to this place, it has in itself proven to be an interesting chapter of equal measures of laughter, gloom and excitement. In the early years, Dennis and I would pack up the car and bomb down to Portsmouth (save a sailor week) and board the ferry to either La Rochelle or Le Harve. It was those days when, still setting the place up, you needed to be constantly taking stuff across, so planes were out of the question. Like any new project, the place was very liveable but needed attention constantly, especially at wintertime when the place may not be quite so welcoming. Open fires seem all romantic until you have to make sure you have a wood store sufficiently full to do its job as any fire open to the elements with no wood burner to guide and control it means you are constantly refuelling it about ever hour. Yes, even in France the weather isn't perfect. In the early years I think it took its toll on Dennis as there was always something to repair or change and improve. Neither of us, me in particular, were any do-it-yourself buffs.

Painting masonry is a tedious job and getting workmen, as all who try to do so abroad will know, is not always so easy, but we managed and survived it. We used to go there up to four or five times a year in the first few years, making small improvements all the time, yet having to start all over again on returning. Viv and Gordon had delivered the second-hand, discarded home furniture in the first few months of settling there and it did its service for a few more years.

Then terror struck in one year when Dennis overfilled the engine oil and 60 miles into the journey from the UK to the port we chugged to a halt and had to call The AA. We missed the ferry, had to return home and start all over next day. This second journey saw another tribulation, with a punctured tyre somewhere into the journey at a similar spot to the last incident. This time, in pouring soaking rain, we made it to the ferry five minutes prior to embarkation, knackered and sweaty - not a pretty sight. Then the obligatory five-hour drive to the cottage to be met with no door key, usually located in the barn. Dennis had to prise open a window and climb into what seemed like a black out, seeing a black-hole horror of thousands of flies embedded and living in a huge blanket of what seemed millions on the walls, all alive and well. Me, demented in the courtyard demanding a gin and Pimms and refusing to move until they were all dispatched somehow to Hell. I am not difficult or demanding am I? Poor Dennis. No wonder his vision regarding country life in the depths of rural France were somewhat at odds with mine.

I sat outside at 4am and drank a large gin as Dennis somehow sprayed and lit fires to burn the offending winged filth to another world. Brushing them up and into the eternal flames, he then checked the bedrooms for remaining occupants, made me a bed then put me into it, heavily veiled, till again he must have risen early to destroy any remaining vampires from hell, with a mug of hot tea and a dishevelled face telling me all was clear and safe. No wonder he was to finish any love affair with France as he came to associate it as being just as demanding and as difficult as me.

Over the next few years, Ken Davies, my old friend, often without his dear wife Wendy would accompany me there. Wendy was not so keen on the French location or life as she had in her youth lost her sister to a fatal and tragic road accident there. I am sure it must have held painful associations for her though she has visited, and subsequently so. Also, her two delightful girls have stayed there, now being two fully-fledged young ladies.

It was around the early part of 2002 and Viv decided she loved the idea of France and staying at the house, knowing by then that Dennis was not at all so interested in going again. So an arrangement was made that she became involved herself and Dennis was happy to relinquish any financial hold with the venture. Also, Gordon is an amazing builder of the old school, you know the type that used to turn up, complete the task and produce craftsmanship and quality. Knowing that, from now on, this house would be given even more of a makeover. After yet more disastrous events there of leaking roofs and getting workmen to rip us off, I knew we were in safe hands from now.

Whilst Dennis was still alive we did make more visits there, the four of us, and he was more relaxed and rested knowing he wouldn't have me on his back to groan and moan. In fact his last time there was the Christmas time of 2003 after his graveyard incident. He did seem to unwind and relax and that pleased me as we were able to look after him and he was happy to potter around with no responsibility on his shoulders for the house.

In the years of 2009 and 2010, major work has been undertaken, with the barns being virtually rebuilt and still in progress to make even more delightful space, with a little 'Bunny Edge' for myself to escape any hustle and bustle I may not wish to engage with. Although this rebuilding is slow, as it is mainly only Gordon's undertaking, the quality of his craftsmanship is inspiring. The French, in their older buildings, do not have proper insulation, either on walls or roof, so to ensure we are a freezing-free zone, painstaking work is in progress to make sure this house will have all the modern comforts to spend an old age in warmth at wintertime.

We now adopt the philosophy that we don't surround ourselves with things and possessions we don't like. We throw them out and have only things that are pleasing to the eye or we wish to be surrounded by. We only like things of beauty darlings. My life today is combined with good fortune, time and the love of old friends, so a lucky fellow I am. I am told all of our homes have been happy places to be in and the warmth of our friendships and laughter over the years have made this all possible.

Even as Dennis lay unwell and toward the end, he was quietly asking our inner circle if they would look out for me and ensure I looked after myself when he was gone. I believe he was reassured in all these requests as he really must have been so concerned for my coping abilities after his death, but for both him and me I shall ensure I do take good care the best I can in order to keep his spirit alive.

*****

CHAPTER 14

My friend Ken Davies and his wife Wendy as mentioned have always been in my life since 1970. One amusing anecdote regarding Ken and Dennis was the year Dennis was to die. Ken was always available to help me or Dennis out if my occasional work and Dennis's hospital appointments clashed, even though he would have to drive from Wellingborough to Birmingham for it. He was always at hand at a moment's notice.

Whilst working away, I asked him to take Den for a special investigation and test to Heartlands Hospital (I often called it heartless). Ken related to me afterwards that Den was a bit irritable and was obviously in pain and found it all an effort. As Ken was attempting to park carefully, Dennis was to cry out, "GOODNESS, YOU DRIVE LIKE A BLOODY OLD WOMAN. YOU COULD GET A TANK IN THAT SPACE. JUST LIKE AN OLD WOMAN!"

"But Dennis dear I am an old woman. I am actually older than you", retorted Ken with a rye smile.

In 2005, the year of Dennis's death, I don't know how or where the energy stemmed from but a concert in his memory was arranged at a venue called Fonteyn's in Birmingham, very near to the Hippodrome. I undertook this some nine months after his death with proceeds for the Marie Curie hospice. Not having performed for some two years, apart from an occasional burst of ten minutes, this was to be an almost two-hour event if the audience could stand it, and yes they did. As always, under-rehearsed, besides too much of that I may lose my spontaneity!

I was amazed at the turnout for him, as I walked onto the cabaret floor, expecting to perform head-on into the faces of an audience. I was confronted with a room full of people, also standing around the edges and bar area with not a seat to be had. I quickly had to adapt my act to this new arrangement, in order to keep the 'fans' engaged, twirling and walking around to meet all the gazes I could. Dressed in evening suit, I had put on a young girl dancer in a ballet-style modern interpretation of movement which went down well. Thank you Loren. Her performing arts course has paid off well for her as she has entered the profession wholeheartedly with, I am sure, no thanks to me. I camped it up, sang a few songs, even remembering the words! No mean feat! For me, anyway. And my old friend Paul was on hand to raise a few more pounds with raffle prizes of theatre tickets and a champagne dinner for two. Oh what a gay day! Yes I also did a tribute to Larry and to Dorothy and even the young folk stayed the course. The warmth of that audience was not only for me but for you know who, Dennis. Thank you to all for helping us through the evening in celebration of his life. I am not putting myself around much now and besides, I am not so hungry to achieve fame, especially reaching 60! Besides, there is nothing so sad as an ageing wannabe.

Most of my friends have wicked sense of humours.

Jonathan Owen, an actor friend who will be mentioned later by Bill Buckley, he of the four of us who strutted our stuff with the sedan chair at the Birmingham Hippodrome is no exception. Now in advanced years, but younger than me, we all have to revolve our visits to him around his afternoon nap. I call him the 'sleeping beauty'. I wish someone would give him a big kiss to make it easier to visit during late afternoons, but no way will he miss his rest. The phones are switched off, doors locked and down in his bunker he goes. Even his agent will know never to disturb this ritual, not that any response would be forthcoming. So, *'Coronation Street'*, if you want him back do phone in the morning please!

Two other friends, Neil and Peter, I have known for a long time and a few years ago, having been together for over 35 years, they decided to go public and have the civil partnership ceremony. I was asked to make a short speech back at their home to the assembled guests who were there to celebrate this incredible partnership. So I did. For me it was a most moving experience, as my reflection on their life together was more poignant after losing Dennis to cancer.

Peter is a talented actor and puppeteer although his art has given way to a generation of animatronics. He made Hollywood films using this craft, operating some daunting technical work with mechanical devices being worked by him in close quarters with the stars as large as a brick house! Working on the film *'Lost in Space'* and working very close with one star Matt Le Blanc was I think quite a sweaty encounter for him! His partner Neil is head of a department in further education, doing good things under remarkable pressures - a very stressful occupation to be in, I know. Both of us have had some great fun nights out and their hospitality and generosity has been offered over the years. They are two very loved individuals to all who know them.

*****

Reflecting over the years, I was thinking of the late actress Doris Hare who lived till she was 95 up to the year 2000. I had been invited to a function at the Variety Artists Ladies and Children's Guild by the then secretary June Groves. Doris, along with many others, like the fantastic actress Lynda Baron, were also in attendance. Doris was into her 80s then. She was a joy with her deep-toned voice and she was a lively actress and still treading the boards. She had been awarded the MBE as far back as 1941 for her services to the business, but was always best remembered by the public as the mother in that most popular TV series *'On The Buses'*. We spent a long time chatting and she was funny and as interested in me as I was in her. She had hailed from Wales and remembered her roots fondly, having trod the boards from such a young age, first appearing in her parents' portable theatre in South Wales at the age of three. She went on to make films and appear in everything from Pinter plays and light-hearted farce to the Royal Shakespeare Company.

If there was anything she hadn't done in the theatre I don't know what it was. One thing she did turn down was the iconic role of Ena Sharples in *'Coronation Street'*, leaving the door open for Violet Carson. We talked and I probed, as fascination of actors has always been my want. She was remarkably forthcoming. We even exchanged contacts but, shortly after she moved into Denville Hall and we lost touch. I regret not going to see her there.

A superb performance by Lynda Baron was delivered in the docudrama *'The Road to Coronation Street'*. Although undoubtedly nervous of playing Violet Carson, Ena Sharples in *'The Street'*, she delivered the most outstanding performance that is the talk of the profession and many others not connected to the business. When will she be more formally recognised as the brilliant actress she is?

*****

My love of art has only really taken hold in the last dozen years or so. It's a very subjective and personal passion. I believe if it fires your visual senses then it's doing its job. Not always am I attracted to pretty pictures of thatched cottages, rural scenes and the like. I had that phase shaped by what I thought I should like and it also being mainly what I had been exposed to. The more Victorian and 18th and 19th century original art is often very expensive and not my taste. I found that, when I had funds, I was drawn to contemporary, often British and northern, art - also abstracted pieces and expressionism.

Many northern artists of the 20th century, some still living, have made some amazing contributions and a lot of it is still affordable. The most well known is probably L S Lowry and even he had to wait till he was approaching old age to get some recognition, which he of course did and, amazingly so, in his lifetime.

To see the work of these artists today is still an inspiring experience. I think most of Britain is lulled into the belief that these high street popular galleries offer the best available art. I don't believe they do. They mainly serve to rip off the artist with a huge mark up and work him or her to death, often under duress to produce an extortionate amount of work, which they run off in so called 'limited edition' prints. To make their killing with very little real reward for the artist.

Some of these artists have been conned into signing away their freedoms, with the response from these exploitative owners that they are making them well known to the public. Yet when they fall out of favour, they will stop producing their work and are not free to pursue other outlets. They are, in effect, in a stranglehold. To control an artist in this way is extortionate and dishonourable; tantamount to bordering on illegal. Artists should challenge what are, in effect, unfair contracts, or just not sign anything once or if they ever get free. I have seen these unfair contracts and the effect they have on the freedom of the individual. This system can perpetuate contempt and unfairness. Some gallery organisations are better than others, but most of them have no real love of art or the artists they promote. Some are happy to go along with it but many fear standing up for a fairer system of freedom over their own work.

One such artist is the amazing Sarah-Jane Szikora. She has made a stand and has the respect of many too scared to speak out. It has been a costly time for her, both financially and emotionally, but I know she will negotiate through it and become even stronger and more successful due to her struggle. Her art is very unique and modern and diverse. If any of you have seen her original pieces then you will know what I mean. Fat people, often women, a celebration of a kind that dominate her canvas. Humour is integral to her pictures - her mind dissects humour like a razor and her output is often vivid and bright but also experimental and challenging and always raising a smile.

You do, to appreciate them, need to be expansive in your thoughts and likes as they are not a typical country scene in any way. Jammy dodgers, biscuit men, angels, devils, shopaholics, cakes, sweets, ice cream and all the human pleasures, together with exotic thin or fat angels are cleverly woven into a picture. Some are elegant, some are scary, some are laughable but always brilliant. Go get a print at least if you can find one or treat yourself to an original direct from the artist herself. Now she is free from her corporate chains, Sarah only produces very controlled numbers of her print runs, as prior to this the opportunists would print far too many of which she had no control over.

The artist Sarah-Jane Szikora inspired me to write these ramblings and threatened to illustrate them! She has been an inspiration to me since meeting her in the late 90s. I have watched her grow as an artist and as a person, her pictures posses a unique sense of the ridiculous with a sense of seriousness and surprise in message. Her range, content and imagination to me and countless others, offer a delight and joy to see. It is what art should be - accessible and unusual. It is thoughtful and humorous and reactionary and does its job to the observer. She has countless fans and buyers for her unique pieces, and will surprise you each time she evolves yet another picture from her studio. She also fought many battles with the art establishment. At last, she is seeing some positive reward for her energies having been put in an impossible position but has now almost succeeded in her ultimate goal of complete independence over her own creative works. Hopefully she will complete her own book soon to warn other aspiring artists of the pitfalls of being controlled by exploitative publishers and galleries, only to fall foul of

The late, wonderful Doris Hare, she of *'On the Buses'*.

With Lynda Baron at The Ladies' Guild.

them when you are out of favour - a replacement and inferior competitor is signed up to keep you in your place.

Sarah-Jane Szikora was born in County Durham (she's still a young wench) into a half Hungarian family. Always fond of drawing from a very young age, with a liking for hopscotch. Like a lot of young folk she couldn't wait to leave school and start her real education for life. It was around 1987 when her first fatties and thinnies came to life, leaving art school in 1991 creating all sorts of artistic funnies, often featuring large ladies with tiny heads. She also creates an avalanche of other funnies with themes of food, animals, cats in particular, shoes, angels and devils, gingerbread people, biscuits and cakes to make them all come alive and stimulate the viewer's mind. In the mid 90s her buxom ladies were published and followed by hundreds of interestingly-shaped characters in equally mind-blowing situations. What this woman can do with a Smartie or a jelly baby has to be seen to be believed! This woman can think way outside any box and the bigger the box the bigger her mind expands. She never ceases to amaze with her creations, they are and deserve to be in the very best of collections. She is the best.

Other works by artists that I admire are that of William Ralph Turner - very much a northern expressionist of such diversity and often inspired by German expressionists - his work is becoming widely appreciated. And very collectable. Fred Yates, now dead, often produced some real potboilers but his use of simple figures and colour are truly wonderful.

Don McKinley, another northern artist who, though loving the female nude, does some very intriguing work of varied variety including landscape and interiors and gossipy pubs and people in abstracted ways in a loose and delicate form. Sue Atkinson, another of this group, is inspired by the northern life and influences of people that are often merry or dancing or walking a coastal path, or a farmer and his dogs - a vast repertoire of situations and touch are brought to her palate and conveyed with colour and skill.

Geoffrey Key and his almost draughtsman-like pieces are bold and decisive and cover a range of situations from musicians to places abroad, like Amsterdam, the rural north and China. People and still life are produced with equal effect. Peter Stanaway and Reg Gardner are another two very different artists of the north who are producing good, substantial and desirable works. One other artist whose work is almost abstract in nature in his perceptions, is Derek Balmer. Though not of the north he is as equally diverse and original.

So even a working class lad like me can appreciate such things, as some of these works do so much represent a past industrial time that has vanished, but stays in the memory of those of a generation who recall it. Sometimes, that lost little boy will see in these pictures those memories evoked of that bygone age that still stand in ruins or were demolished, starting in the 70s and 80s. These leftovers from a century of the industrialisation of the north and the Midlands were hard work and a no-nonsense attitude prevailed, in order to deal with those days of hardship. It reminds me that those hardships endured by my adopted parents and their generation did also produce some decent values of self worth and community that has all but vanished. Well there is my rant about art and its effect on me to date.

*****

Being a homosexual man may, for some, produce a feeling of unease but not for me. It seemed a natural evolution and generally a positive experience. It's all determined by your early experiences and attitudes. For some they are negative and produce turmoil and conflict, for others it is a life-enhancing experience that is not just about sexual activity (but that's nice too). No doubt I fit the latter description.

So many theories abound and I don't hold fast to any of them as it's not important to know a cause as though it needs rationalising and theorising. Causation can hark back to those dark days of when it was described as an illness and, amazingly, some belief is held regarding this by the 'unnatural brigade'. There are theories for all human motivation and behaviours as to why anything occurs. They are based on either a psychodynamic, social, behavioural model or a medical, biological and genetic model. Frankly darlings, I Don't give a fruitcake.

The extreme right wing of orthodoxy will never approve, but then I don't approve of them. I don't need them to validate my experience and life despite any judgments made on its worthwhileness or value. I have never been an active campaigner but I have always recognised the right to make choices with equal treatment of all and fairness in all area of life, where consideration is given for people's diversity. I am no different to many other open and fair-minded people. We should not be judged for sexual interests and appetites, providing those who experience them are not damaging or influencing others in any harmful way. If you or I am to care for someone who needs assistance and comfort should own personal sexuality come between those parties when help is needed? I like to believe that a rounded life experience may be helpful in the quest to assist others at times of ill health or vulnerability. I say this as a nurse and an individual in the genuine belief that we can all make a difference to people's lives.

Perhaps my way of coping with life's traumas and unpleasantness has been to be that occasional comedian who sees the madness in it all and needs to express it into laughter. For sometimes, the audience and the performer need it. Some may not like it, some may take offence, but some will see the joke and laugh along at the stupidity of it all. As for when I read the countless horror stories of victims of the systems of the past and present where the vulnerable have to seek refuge, I return to Dennis in my mind who taught me to see the suffering in others and that we are not always what we seem. One lesson also that I have learnt through those years in psychiatry to which I will now return.

Acceptance is, I think, what has been the big lesson for me, and it's not easy to achieve this. When someone is hostile or is abusive or bad mouthing you, how do you accept this? In the work within the relationship between patient and nurse you just have to do it. You inform yourself at every moment that this person is unwell, even mad at this moment and it may change. It's that message that helps you accept and it's a hard one to do. Within a life outside of this, it's a greater challenge as you can manage a relationship by either not encouraging it or walk away from it - that's the choice we have. You cannot do this with in a professional one.

*****

Reflecting on those patients that made a great impression on my life and skills I return to someone I will call Annie. I ran a ward called A22 at Rubery hospital in South Birmingham. I was to commission the opening of this new ward. What it actually was set up for was to decant 22 highly difficult, somewhat mixed bunch of gals, that didn't fit in anywhere within this system, from around the hospital and send them to me. I received all the assistance, I needed none.

However, this next two years was to prove the biggest, most eventful passage in my life as a charge nurse. I was to enjoy every moment of it. Most of these women would have been diagnosed with various manifestations of schizophrenia, many of the paranoid and persecutory type. My aim was to reduce over time the amount of medication they were on and to establish new base lines of behaviours and tolerance on the part of the staff. Some challenge in those days.

There was this one lady, Annie, who, when calm, was a delight but her disordered thinking was always near to the surface and she was not able to suppress it for long. She had gathered a reputation as a strangler! Yet I could ascertain no evidence of her doing anyone real sustained harm. Her delusions took on the form that she was being bombed by the Germans, that she was on fire and that abortions were running out of her. She would scream in terror at these 'real' happenings; she could visualise and feel the effect of this experience happening to her. This was her reality on these occasions.

Historically, she had been managed by being given intramuscular anti-psychotic drugs and manoeuvred into a locked side ward with only a mattress on the floor. To be leered and peeped at, to see her settle or otherwise and maybe given food when she was calmer and after medications had taken effect. I intended to change that. I informed the staff what our new regime would be when I was on duty. Two nurses would sit each side of her and hold her hands and talk her down. She was not, under any circumstances, to be taken to the side room. I would be there and would sit with them. If she was to act out in any way, she was not to be dragged, pulled or marched anywhere but we would contain her somehow. Also, no medication was to be attempted to be given till after the incident and that would be discussed.

My students took to this well, some of my older colleagues not so well, but defy me they dare not. I tried to lead by example and went straight to her when she started her frightened, scared shouting and pushing; we took her hands, made her sit and held her and talked calmly but firmly, asking and telling her to look at us. That what was happening was not happening - it would pass, we were there. Sometimes, she would struggle and break loose. We would follow her and get her seated again. We continued this for weeks and never once put her back into that side room. She was expecting it but it never happened on my watch.

As the weeks rolled into months, she became accustomed to this new tactic and seemed easier to manage. Sometimes, she occasionally took a shoe to break a small window. Once she did this and I told the staff to leave her. After breaking the window and looking around at us at the same time at our non-response, I shouted, "Annie, you have missed one there!" Besides, all of the people would now get a little colder tonight with the broken windows. She couldn't get her head around this approach. Eventually her outpourings were limited to around once every two weeks and she was far more controllable. You would call this a form of behavioural modification but with very little punitive action.

Once, I followed her screaming into the corridors but took no action. I was informed to get her back to the ward by a nursing officer. I told him where to go in no uncertain terms. I wasn't so popular with these old establishment figures and I knew with my arrogance and know all I would be fired eventually. This is what institutions did to you. Though I had supporters amongst these ranks.

I was also to take Annie out on a bus for the first time maybe in over 20 years. I wondered if she would let me down and gave much preparation to it, involving her at every stage of the planning - such a simple task you may think but a huge stride for her. I was in receipt of a suit allowance as I did not wear the white coat (or hat) of a nurse. A great stride forward! So, my plan was to take Annie on a bus to a local tailor in the next suburb, fit myself with a suit and return hopefully in one piece with the suit.

All went well for the first part. I took her on the bus and she seemed calm and interested. We entered the shop. She followed me and I consulted her on choice. We agreed a pin stripe. She seemed a little agitated, some of the signs of her blowing were imminent. I did the deal as quick as I could and we left the store with her face grimacing as we exited. I reassured her we just had a short bus ride back and asked her to behave as best she could on the bus, in fact I pleaded with her.

There were a few strange looks and expressions of horror by now on both our faces. I rang the bell and we exited the bus one stop short and alighted quickly. She was about to explode I thought. Talking to her quietly all the way, we walked and entered the hospital grounds. She erupted like Mount Vesuvius! Well at least we were inside the hospital grounds. I put my arm firmly around her, holding the other close to my side and scurried into the ward. We were both perspiring, me more than her. It must have been a distressing time for her to have achieved so much. This time I did give her the PRN medication to help her relax. I insisted she lay on her bed for an hour. A few noises and a sharp eye kept on her. She seemed to calm once more and the rest of the day passed without incident. Lucky me! I related the trip to the other staff who must have thought I was more bonkers than Annie and a learning session evolved from the incident. This to me was a big step on the road to rehabilitation, which would be long way off.

Ironically, some six or seven months later, Annie took hold of the lapel on this same suit and proceeded to tear it off (quite neatly as it happened), almost completely severing it from the main body of the jacket. Well it was not my body after all, just a suit. Some months later even she was to laugh at the madness of it all.

*****

I still see all these, what appear small moments, as huge leaps forward to the normalisation of people with severe mental illness. We must remember that these were times when community care sprang from the institutional wards of these old Victorian piles. It had to start somewhere - it started here.

Recalling these almost halcyon days (no pun intended Sarah-Jane), I am now reminded of Elsie. After a period as a tutor in the School of Nursing, I decided to practise what I had preached and returned to the clinical areas. The first year of the return was at a Community Mental Health resource centre called Radford Road in Leamington Spa, one of only 14 such projects nationwide at that time. It provided a crisis walk-in centre, individual and group psychotherapy. It was dynamic and set up to prevent wholesale alternatives to hospitalisation. After that I returned to run an admission ward that was named, as I mentioned earlier, Jane

Austen, to be followed to another intensive care environment called William James, an area where those who were so disturbed by their distress were admitted, usually on a section, to be 'helped', to be stabilised. It was at this time that Elsie was to figure in my life. I returned to another admission ward where I met her.

Agitated depression is a pitiful and excruciating sight to witness. It is where the person again has a severe delusional mood, producing morbid wretched gloom with the added dimension of unproductive negative energy. So you see the morbid person but they are talking and moving in ever increasing and diminishing circles of misery. They talk with morbid high anxiety, which is expressed in the conversation that is usually one-sided with the content of gloom and despair.

Elsie was a sufferer of this. She couldn't sleep. Imagine the mindset of this person. How could they rest? So sedation is used often for the peace of others but to little effect. With the view of attempting to give the person some respite from the terrible state they are in. She would wander down the ward before 7am, sometimes as early as 4am. The empty house bemoaning her plight.

"Look at this. I have got no clothes, I can't eat. What can I do? My God, I should be dead. Oh my God, here am. I shouldn't be here, I've got no clothes, no home, no money. What to do?"

This misery never abated - it was there in some form all day every day. It was not uncommon to have at least two or even three other sufferers in mutual misery throughout a stay, often lasting up to nine months before any noticeable improvement was evident and still then, always bubbling under the surface. You can see that this profound endogenous type of depression needs hospitalisation as they could not or can not survive in a community setting. People's understanding of this type of depressive illness is still somewhat naive to say the least. Though it's doubtful they would ever witness it - only perhaps at a very early onset.

This tortured little wizened face would greet me in the morning of an early shift, often half dressed with knickers being shown to me - twanging of the elastic and rummaging around uncomfortably, and often inside out or the wrong way round! To reinforce the belief she had no clothes. Whilst I was setting up for the day to give the staff a break from her constant demands and misery, I would have her with me in the office and just listen to her woes by non-verbal acknowledgement, even sometimes agreeing with her.

At least while I was encouraging her to sit still, she was at least resting in a sitting position. With my firm commands each time she got up to, "Sit back there Elsie and hang on and wait for me." For up to half an hour I would attempt to contain her in this situation, then walk her to breakfast at a table on her own and ensure something went into her stomach.

One morning I entered the ward to find her almost naked, running towards me. As I stopped, looked and reinforced my disapproval at her lack of attire I said, "Elsie... What on earth are you doing?"

"I am ready to go on Tom Bunn's fun run", was her firm and instant reply. I just broke down into fits of laughter at this inane comment, totally unsolicited. I even noticed a smirk of a wry smile from Elsie. How do you not see the amazing side of these individuals, as even in misery there is constant humour?

She did improve and was discharged, probably over a history of at least five other times. She would have a reasonable quality of life for up to 18 months, then return for yet another revolving readmission. The tragedy of this particular manifestation is that its onset is often in the middle years, so not only are they having to live with this misery, combined with this unhealthy energy, they have the added disadvantages of increasing old age. This burns them out. At this age, the illness can be complicated with a host of physical problems to be managed as well, as it is the age we all start to encounter other medical complications. As it is combined often with quite large doses of medications, it is most important to maintain constant vigilance on the physical condition, diet and hydration.

Poor sweet old Elsie. My last decade in the NHS and psychiatry saw me part of that team that helped embed the community services into a structured, integrated service, being the head of Clinical and Professional Development for the then stand-alone Mental Health Trust, This eventually became a large community trust, losing out somewhat in its speciality and identity. Under the watchful leadership of Jo Carver, our Chief Executive, she steered the transition successfully by getting the services in place well before any of the previous services were dismantled.

I have great respect for Rene and her team then as they were committed, focused and, due to their energies and focus, they laid not only the foundations of a progressive service but they did it with the care and enthusiasm through a difficult period of national and local change in South Warwickshire. I was proud to play my small part in this. Rene Mathieu, the then Director of Nursing, was a stalwart support throughout the whole change programme. We had some light-hearted days together. Jo and I both had wicked senses of humour and were often ensconced in a room ripping everything to shreds to lighten the load. She was a workaholic and, now in her seventies, continues to work outside and undertake work in the gardens of a grand castle or house, probably Brodick Castle, if my memory serves me correctly, on the Isle of Arran in Scotland, where she eventually decided to root herself.

*****

CHAPTER 15

A few years before all of this, I got a small part in a wonderful TV series called *'Gods Wonderful Railway'*. One of its stars was the enigmatic Brian (booming) Blessed. The location shots and filming were undertaken around the Clee Hills near to Ludlow. These hills form a gateway from the West Midland to the Shropshire borders and mid Wales and span north-south for over 15 miles. It was summertime and we were halfway up some mountain, creating the illusion of building the railway tracks digging out the Great Western Railway line.

Such fun this proved to be, as the crowd I was with were a close bunch of jobbing extras much like me at the time, always hoping we may get picked for a more substantial scene. It was great fun holding big butch sledge hammers and camping it up until the director would shout, "Action!", and the butch side had to be brought in to play. On my part, that meant swinging a pickaxe and sweating like a bull, dressed in hot Victorian workman's clothes that included an old battered top hat. Really, I ask you! No wonder we perspired and it looked authentic.

Brian Blessed is good fun and was a joy in keeping his own and others spirits up on set. Somehow, when I was talking of the late Mrs Shufflewick earlier, I was also reminded of the other great unstoppable act of the drag Marc Fleming. Both of these two worked together and very little material can be found on them. They were so very different in style. Marc you loved or hated. He was truly insulting and very rude and the chance of TV never came his way until the delightful toned-down version of Paul O'Grady doing his Lily Savage.

Many a person attending the London gay scene of the 60s and 70s would have been treated to a tirade from Marc at some point. He was the master of making an audience excruciate themselves in pain with his amazing tirade on the audience, politicians and the royal family at a time when the royals were not lampooned.

Fleming would say, "Charles, the next Queen of England", and Princess Anne was a, "horse dressed as a woman." If you caught his eye or you were a friend of someone he wanted to put down, his quips and insults flew out like a manic on speed. If easily offended, you stayed away. You had to see it to believe it but those folks loved him. Offstage, he was kind and personable but when those frocks went on the vile tongue of Master Fleming became full throttle, there was no one to touch him.

Here are a few examples of his incredible tirades. Unrepeatable and politically very incorrect but there we go. A woman who dared to heckle when in full throttle would be treated to, "Shut the fuck up you fucking bucket-mouthed hairy lesbian. When I say shit, jump on the shovel."

Another time he would walk on stage, look around the audience, clamber into the seated crowd and state firmly, "There are two things I cant stand, that's prejudice of any type and black bastards", and at the time of saying he would be perched on the lap of a dark-skinned gent, possibly of Asian origin! Talk about Bernard Manning!

He always was topical. Once, there was a time when Mrs Golda Meir, who was the current Israeli prime minister, had been visiting Germany and spoke to the then Chancellor, Willy Brandt. This event had been covered on TV. Marc spat out that she, "Was going to Germany to settle up the gas bill." It may have sickened many but the irony of it was that Marc was Jewish. It may have been his own way of disapproving of the nature of Israel becoming too close with Germany.

My favourites were when he took the naughty out of the Royals by doing a routine so descriptive, describing in grand detail the Queen Mother dressed in black motor cycle leathers, riding her Harley Davidson at a ton down the Mall and around the streets of London. Bedecked with bunches of cherries tied to her helmet, smashing all the traffic lights with a hammer as she burnt past other traffic screaming and demented, waving her hammer and cussing at the top of her voice. Arriving at Buckingham Palace to dog-sit while Queen Elizabeth was at a function, his descriptions of her slipping off her boots, flicking and turning on the TV with her toe whilst searching out the Dubonet for the gin and crawling on hands and knees to find it from the bottom of drinks cabinets was hilarious. Especially when the news presenter at ITN *'News at Ten'* announced, "Now we go over live to Clarence House to speak with the Queen Mother", as she spits out her gin and with obscenities and expletives to make her exit for Clarence House. This character may have horrified many, but he packed them out at a time when TV would never have taken such a risk and it appealed to an audience to see the powerful and famous pilloried this way. In a live setting it was memorable.

TV has now acclimatised us and, in particular, the younger of the audiences, to some good stuff maybe, but the dearth of shows transmitted today could never transplant those memories of these entertainers I encountered along my journey. You may not approve perhaps of these performers' remarks and I don't say I condone it, but thank goodness I was just around to see them.

*****

In most of these years I would meet and see other performers deliver their goods. Dennis hardly ever accompanied me but relived as usual these exploits at some stage after the event. I met another stage-struck person who is an amazing chap, kind, considerate and always on hand to give a helping hand - George Lapper, now happily living in Spain with his partner. As a complete opposite to his job as a bus driver and going around inner and outer circles all his life, George has combated this long affair with buses by entertaining anywhere and everywhere he could. He made a lovely drag queen and songstress, and loves the thrill of tarting himself up at any opportunity as an Andrew Sister with a bunch of others. He was the most buxom one there and did on a few occasions join me and introduced me on stage. Thank you George.

Bill Buckley, he of the former *'That's Life'* programme, can testify that I did resort to some naughty moments in those days myself. Here is his account of our first meeting and him becoming my musical director before he was to go on to be a presenter with Esther Rantzen on that well-loved series.

First meeting:

Bunny and I first met backstage at the Birmingham Hippodrome. I was a wet behind the ears 20-year old from polite suburbia who had never encountered anything like this flamboyant, effervescent and downright loud creature. I was instantly captivated.

He and I were half of a four-man team, dressed in footmen's wigs and breeches, who were to carry a sedan chair containing a dancer from the Royal Ballet onto the stage. She would emerge, pirouette for a few minutes whilst we stood stock still, get back into the chair, and we would trundle her off again. It was a brilliant gig; it required no talent and only a few moments of physical effort. What's more, the spot came early in the show, so within half an hour of curtain up, we were free to go. And it paid well too, £9 per performance, two on the Friday, two on the Saturday.

One of the other chair carriers was, coincidentally, Jonathan, a mutual friend. As we waited to do our stuff for the final time on Saturday night, Bunny took him and me on one side, away from the fourth corner of the sedan chair, a very dull family man with whom none of us had gelled.

"Now, listen," Bunny commanded, "by the end of tonight, we will each have earned £36 we weren't expecting. This is what we are going to do: we are going to the Midland Hotel where I happen to know champagne cocktails are £3 each. We shall buy a round. We are not allowed to order the same thing twice. We shall try each others drinks, thereby tasting nine champagne cocktails for only £9. We will still each have £27 to put in the bank so it isn't extravagant and anyway, darlings, we deserve it after lugging that f**king chair back and forth in this ridiculous get-up!"

Soon, we were on our way. Bunny made his entrance to the Midland, a very posh and rather staid bar, pausing at the door to survey the scene with a Dietriech-esque ironic eyebrow, then swishing his long leather coat back and forth as we descended down the stairs with Jonathan hissing, "Bunny, stop it, you will have us thrown out!"

I was too shocked to say anything but was loving every minute of it. I thought of my mum and dad who were almost certainly watching the telly at that moment in their nice, safe, suburban home with a nice cup of tea as they did every night. How they would have disapproved of my friend, flamboyantly drawing attention to himself for which there was no excuse. And how they would have hated their boy mixing with 'one of that type' -

I had already come out to them but it was just a phase as far as they were concerned which mixing with the likes of Bunny (and what kind of name is that for a man?) could only exacerbate and prolong.

Anyway, we each bought our round and sipped each other's cocktails - and three rounds later, it was time to go home. None of us had eaten, I was inexperienced in the ways of alcohol, and I have no memory at all from about halfway through the drinking session until I woke next morning. I had miraculously found my way, unharmed, back to the grotty flat I shared in Moseley (Birmingham's bed-sit land). I had made it into the right bed but was still fully dressed!

I felt terribly pleased with myself - awfully Bohemian - and didn't even have a hangover.

Gimme shelter:

Not long after I met Bunny, I met someone else, my first love. We will call him Leroy, for Leroy is not his name.

I, you will recall, was a 20-years old, butter wouldn't melt, white boy from the comfy suburbs. Leroy was black, 26, working class, and, having realised his true sexual orientation rather late, a separated father of three. He had a council flat, and was a factory worker by day and a male stripper by night. In short, he was everything my parents weren't looking for in a partner for their only son. This, of course, made him irresistible. For a while, we were giddily in love.

There was, however, a fly in the ointment by the name of Simon (also not his name). Simon had been Leroy's live-in lover for three years and was unceremoniously dumped for me. He was terribly civilised about it, still popping round to see Leroy now and then, and attending the same parties that we did without any awkwardness.

However, at one such gathering, he drank too much, and all his pent-up pain came pouring out. "You've ruined my life!" he slurred, putting his hands around my throat and squeezing with all his might. He was too strong for me, and I thought my number was up. I was so shocked the world went into slow motion. All around me, guests danced, drank, smoked and laughed in slow motion, impervious to my fate as I silently mouthed, "Help!" Finally, a couple of guys realised what was happening and dragged Simon off. Life snapped back to its normal speed and I fled, gasping, into the night.

I was too frightened to go home as Simon knew my address and I thought he might come round and finish the job. But where could I go to instead? I had only left home a few months before. All my school friends were away at university and I didn't feel I could land myself on the few acquaintances I had made since. Going to my mum and dads' or my auntie and uncles' would have involved the third degree grilling. I could only think of Bunny and his partner Dennis's cosy little cottage in Acocks Green.

"You've got to take me in, someone is trying to murder me!" was my opening gambit when they answered the door. And they did, despite the fact we had only met a couple of times. With all the emotion of a true young princess in a taste of shock that I could muster, I rang Leroy and said, "I am starting a new life at a secret address (all four miles from his flat) you'll never find me. Its goodbye forever!" then collapsed, sobbing, at having to give up the man I loved in order to survive. It was a moment of melodrama, which I like to think Bunny himself would have been hard pressed to better. How proud he must have been of his young apprentice.

I lived with him and Dennis for a couple of weeks. They were perfect hosts. Bunny regaled me with scandalous stories. I even got to speak to the legendary operatic comedienne Joan Turner when she rang up for a chat. Dennis meanwhile, kind, down-to-earth homemaking, long suffering Dennis fed me delicious meals and got stuck into the washing up as Bunny, champagne glass in hand, launched into another salacious tale.

After a couple of weeks, Simon somehow acquired their phone number. Leroy, he said, was missing me terribly and would I please come back to him. "But I can't!" I cried, instinctually seizing another opportunity for high drama. "You might kill me." He apologised and swore he would never do it again. And I was eventually persuaded. Back I went and all was well.

It was good to be back in the strong dark arms of the man I loved, although I missed Bunny's tales of Larry Grayson and Dorothy Squires, not to mention Dennis's hearty stews and sponge pudding.

For a while, Bunny and I were not just friends but professional colleagues. He was doing comedy one-nighters around the Midlands and I became his musical director. 'Musical Director' was a pretty fanciful name for it: I played him on at the start (using a few bars I wrote specially) on my electric keyboard, then accompanied the five or six songs he scattered through his act. Basically, the songs were there to give him thinking time, whenever his patter started to falter he would cue the next number.

We played women's-only nights at everywhere from small pubs to the vast British Leyland social club in Longbridge, where several hundred braying women turned up to be scandalised by Bunny's blue gags. Dressed as a giant rabbit in fishnets and proper fur tail, he opened with, "Hello, girls. I feel ever so relaxed tonight. I've just stretched me twat over a dustbin." The howls of delighted outrage at this frankly foul remark were deafening. I had never encountered women like these before, my mother rarely raised her voice, never swore and hardly drank, whilst this lot were louder and dirtier than men. This young Sutton Coldfield boy was learning about life, and learning fast.

More than 20 years later, I came back to Birmingham for the weekend to see Bunny perform a night of comedy at a small theatre. The fishnets and bobtail had turned into an immaculate suit, whist whimsical and only mildly risqué material had been replaced the bluer-than-blue gags, as befitted the more mixed-gender and altogether classier audience, and the more salubrious venue. He was still using my play on music though!

Due to my friendship over the years with Bill, I came to know Bobby Crush. A bit of a legend in showbiz circles; that early 70s winner of *'Opportunity Knocks'* has gone on to do many performances and show his talents. One of his latest creations, a special piece written for him has been *'Liberace at the Gates of Heaven'*, having played in the West End with this show and touring abroad to great acclaim and demonstrating his own skill as a brilliant pianist and as an actor with both pathos and humour. The voice of God in the production is provided by Victoria Wood and St Peter by Stephen Fry. It's a super piece to indulge yourself in. Particularly, as the story unfolds you, the audience, vote either into hell or into heaven dear old Liberace himself. We still meet up when life permits and he is a joy to be around.

*****

I am reminded of one show I did in Birmingham. It must have been in the late 70s. Three of us had been approached to appear at some festival show organised by a local DJ. There was the wonderful and naughty 'Midlands most misleading Lady, Ricki Deuvex' - I called her Miss Quilt. We had done a few shows together with the wonderful Tony Page, a well-known London drag entertainer. We were all at this time doing some venues around the Midlands and were all on very friendly terms. As often was, the show was promoted as a charity event and the venue was a large hotel in New Street, then called the Britannia. We all arrived early and had a large hotel room as our dressing room, with reasonable access to the stage but down about three flights of steps. We could hear the crowd and they seemed buoyant and noisy to say the least, most having arrived early.

Usually it's not a good idea to go on as first turn, but as I was going out and peeping out at the crowd prior to the show (unknown to them) I detected a strong sense of inebriation afoot! As Tony would make himself up his persona always changed as he reached for more eye lashes from his make-up box which he called his Tool Box since it was a metal one. We would become more terrified at watching the transformation like a Jekyll and Hyde transition. So the running order was Bunny Thomas, Ricki Deuvex, my all-time favourite, and Tony Page. I seemed to have to wait ages in the wings and I hadn't got time to dash up three flights of stairs to empty the bladder so I have to admit to a desperate move of a stream dribbling down a stairwell. Sorry Britannia.

Out I went and camped it up. I did some gags, desperately trying to get them on my side. One part of the room were obviously pissed, the other half wanting to enjoy the show and you could feel the antagonism in the room. I struggled through 25 minutes, survived, belted into a song and departed the stage in haste. I told my fellow thespians that they were a noisy lot and what I had detected in that room. Ricki was in a state of fear and anxiety yet he was well-used to dealing with the noisy banter of clubland. So on he went. The noise and the tension rose between the now opposing sides of the room between the 'shut up and listen' brigade and the 'shut up and let's wreck the evening' crowd.

About five minutes into his act, a fight broke out at the back of the room. Ricki carried on. He made fun of it but attention had by now turned away from the stage, he cut his spot short and came off. Next, the heavyweight, Tony Page took to the arena. After five minutes into his act, a drunken woman staggered up onto the stage and whispered something into Tony's ear. He screeched back to the audience, "This pisshead has just told me to fuck off. So I will. Good night and fuck off!"

With that we packed our bags and left by a back entrance, running in fear of our lives to our friendly club named The Jug run by the inimitable founder of the gay club scene Laurie Williams, who I will tell you more of later. On entering the safety of The Jug, Laurie consoled us with a few optics of brandy for Tony and a sausage sandwich for Ricki. A large vodka for me saw us all comforted. Methinks my canny decision to go on first that night proved a blessing in disguise.

Well, by now you can see the classy joints I performed in during this period of time. Most successful performers of my generation who made it far bigger than me will all have stories of how tough this game can be and it's often ironic that a lot of them end up where they started. That is what is left of clubland. Well, maybe not all. If they can still stand they either *'Dance on Ice'*, do *'Strictly Come Dancing'* or get on *'Come Dine with Me'*.

Comics and entertainers all develop skills in putdowns and sharp retorts when being heckled or wound up by a noisy or indifferent crowd, or just finding yourself in a tight corner - its true masochism. Sometimes these replies, looking off the cuff, can work or backfire, though if you have the majority with you the banter can be amusing and fun. So many will tell you of these types of situations and maybe you have witnessed them yourselves; to control a stage and take charge is unpredictable. Mine may be old and well used but can still often be effective:

"The last time I heard a mouth as big as yours Lester Piggott was sitting on the back of it." Today it would be another well-known jockey.

"Love your hair. Did you come on a motor bike?"

Taxi driver: "I'll have you there before you know it." "I don't want to be there before I know it. It smacks of dementia to me."

Even daring to say, "Would you mind closing your legs dear? There is a terrible draught up here."

I could go on but these worked for me and if I continue with this it will just deteriorate even more.

*****

CHAPTER 16

In the late 60s I met Helen Grace. She had started as a student nurse and worked her way down to a nursing assistant by the first year. That had happened not because of her lack of talent and ability but pure politics of the day. She had been taken on by the old principal tutor, who had just been usurped by new arrangements and organisational change. The new educational director decided that, as she had not been interviewed by herself, Helen now had to commence again under new conditions, thus reverting to nursing assistant status. Helen was totally put out, a dirty trick. Indeed, as so often happens when egos and individual power games come into play it is always the innocent that suffer.

We became instant friends. She was classy, colourful and quite bizarre - just my kind of girl. She was one of hundreds who could trace her family tree to the disinherited Royal Stuarts - dispossessed in every way. She was at odds with a lot of suburbanites and had even, for one so young, a colourful time to date. At one time, a young thing working in London in various jobs, she fell in love with a big black man. That, as it often happens, turned out to be disastrous.

Her mother, a fiery redhead by then in her 60s, used to preach hell and damnation at Speakers' Corner in London and drew lots of attention to herself with her firm views and strange concepts. She was also a health fanatic carrying with her on her many trips cases of pills, which she willingly prescribed to her unfortunates. Needless to say, Helen and her mother had a very estranged relationship, as preaching to Helen how to live her life was tantamount to treason.

Around the time I was qualifying, I held a big party at my former home in Acocks Green. After this event, where much champagne was drunk and a general good time was had, Helen had a brief liaison with a rather handsome Egyptian doctor. A short time later Helen resigned after some bitter run in with the new chief I mentioned and came a knocking some time later at my door, a desperate woman. She was pregnant and had no intention of getting rid and wanted to see the child born. She had also made her decision that she would have the child adopted. She appeared pragmatic on this, and I knew she was doing what she believed best. It was now that Dennis and I had serious talks regarding this. Dennis was all for taking on the unknown child and raising it as our own. Things were not as liberal as they are today.

It was a tormenting time, we both knew the realities of two working men taking on this responsibility. In fairness, Helen put no pressure on the situation, always insisting the child needed a new beginning without her and would ensure that all would be done to find the right couple to take this on. We looked after Helen and prepared for whatever was to come. We ensured we did all the nursey things to ensure a healthy mum and she lived with us the whole term and beyond. By the time of the birth, Helen had arranged through the hospital the inevitable. On holding this little bundle of joy, Dennis found it hard to let it go. It was a little boy and it tugged hard at our heartstrings to see its departure. She put on a brave face and seemed to cope well. It was, as she knew now, not the time for motherhood. We did not intend to moralise or condemn.

Helen stayed on for a while and decided to take a trip to Spain. She fell in love with a most handsome waiter and they both became proprietors of a restaurant and bar and owners of a beautiful large home there. Thanks to Helen's input, she also had two beautiful boys to show for it. Now grown up into young men for who I am godfather. Eventually Helen divorced the husband who could be cruel and demanding and unfaithful, but it lasted well over 20 years. She still lives in Spain and keeps regular contact with her two grown-up lads. She was a brilliant mother to them and they return her love unconditionally as well as to me - she seems to be at peace. As an adopted person myself, I often wonder what became of her young giveaway and if he ever attempted to trace his origins, but I know it's an issue for the individual to discover truth. Whatever or wherever this young person is (who will be approaching 40 at the time of writing this), here is hoping life has been kind for him.

*****

When I moved in 1987 to the house in Flint Green Road with Dennis those neighbours became an integral part of life. It was our own slightly up-market Coronation Street! Karen, the estate agent, who I told you Dennis painted her garden stones blue. Tom and Gabriele Fraser-Dixon and her mother Edith who, after an unusual amount of time under a hairdryer in the kitchen one evening, fell unconscious and I revived her. It became a standing joke how I had now prolonged her life even more. All their kids are no longer kids any more.

The hospitality, the food, the evenings spent together were always appreciated by me. They often, in impromptu fashion, asked to stay for a nibble. Trish and Pete, we called him 'Perfect Pete' - a handsome man now moved with Trish to Cape Verdi. When I was let down by a very slow builder he came to my rescue and finished fitting my uncompleted kitchen. What that man can do with a lump hammer. And I always thought 'two by one' was an African dictator!

An elderly lady looking like a grand dame in her late 70s named Marjorie. We were to become good friends, sharing ideas and talking for hours, and eventually upsetting her relatives at Christmas as she was invited to us despite pleas from her family. We would get her tipsy on champagne and she would totter back with her heels precariously across the road to bed with me, supporting her as we giggled to her front door. She attended every show I did at the Cannon Hill Arts Centre and would come and watch unusual films that I would tell her about and be propped up on my bed whilst Dennis watched another programme downstairs, she is sadly missed.

*****

When I first met Laurie, I must have been in my late teens and there was a club run by the same owner of the Grosvenor Hotel I talked of before. This venue was called Guys Club. It was in the area where the old market place used to be in Birmingham, not far from the old Repertory Theatre. It was my student days and I went along there on my discovery and journey of education and life. I had only heard of Guys from title tattle from other guys I had encountered. The place seemed quite plush and it was spread over two small floors with the theme of stalactites and stalagmites with a grotto on display, like a deep cavernous room designed to look like a cave and in part painted in white. It was quite atmospheric with some velvet-type awnings and pleasant tables, chairs and small sofas. I sat down near the bar at a table to view its clientele.

At the bar, complete with jet-black hair most probably a wig, was this eccentric-looking gent who everyone was calling Laurie. He seemed to be holding court when someone threw some friendly abuse at him, shouting, "Look at that old fairy there." To which Laurie picked a large straw, waved it dramatically as a wand in the caller's direction and shouted with a wave of the wand, "Vanish!", to be followed with the remark, "Die you old queen", as the wand was now turned into a blow pipe containing a fictitious poisonous dart to be blown in the heckler's direction. "Wonderful", thought I.

What a performer he was. I was to discover Laurie was the virtual founder of what is now a very commercial gay scene in Birmingham. He had, I was told, formed many illicit and illegal drinking clubs and watering holes that had been the forerunners to the clubs of today. His first involvement at an established club was a place called the Victoria I mentioned earlier - that place I first met my Dennis. Dennis knew of Laurie and told me much about him and his generous and eccentric ways. The club that Laurie is best remembered for was his own invention of glitzy seediness called The Jug. Prior to this, he was one of the gang that originally created the Nightingale Club, an existing large venue still today, of which I am an honorary member.

The Jug was unique. Lacking in real sophistication it was heaven to any visitor, regular or wandering. That is if Laurie decided to let you in! It had three versions over the years - for me the most memorable one was in Albert Street. Its licence was partly granted that this club was an equity club for use by the theatrical and variety artists of the day. In the days when, on Sunday, a licence was only forthcoming if food was served, Laurie gave oodles of sausages in gravy on a paper plate to every entrant on Sunday to the club, with a few tinned new potatoes to accompany it. His behaviour was enchanting. The oldest disco bunny in town, his humour and tirades were legendary. He called his clientele 'my babbies'.

One memorable evening, I recall a big fight broke out with two lesbians in some lovers' tiff, one pulling ferociously at the other's hair. Laurie, walking across the floor in black suit with jewelled broach and an earring, swept by and said in a loud voice, "I do like to see my babbies enjoying themselves", walking past, unconcerned or troubled.

Every night, entertainment in some form would happen. When finished, Laurie would get on stage and make a few announcements, talking like a feeble Charles Hawtry with little stage presence but dynamic just to watch all the same. On finishing his presentation he would swing the microphone with a twirl of his head and shout, "Now my ladies, let's get back to D.I.S.C.O!"

I performed there, often getting some written evidence of a contract to turn my red Equity card to a full blue one, a must in those days for full membership.

Dennis told me that, when he was a young boy, he recalled Laurie sitting in the Kardomah coffee shop with watches strapped up his arms, selling them to punters and wheeling and dealing. It must have been an outrageous sight as Laurie's appearance was more that of a tough version of Quentin Crisp. He lived with his long-suffering partner eventually of over 45 years, named Lionel, his rock and anchor, very much as Dennis was mine.

There is much more to Laurie than ever I can convey here. Over the years, I always seemed to command a distant respect from him, as I wasn't one of his regular all-consuming groupies but always polite in the outer circle of his life. We were never close friends as I saw it, yet at the ending of his life he turned to me for support and assistance as I felt he knew he could trust me and not let him down. His fortunes had turned around by now. Lionel had died of throat cancer and he went to live in a small rented house not so far from me. He had sold out his last venture, called Laurie's International, a place that never attracted so many customers as if he didn't like the look or sound of you he wouldn't let you in!

I had seen him walking one day a couple of years before and had taken him home to ours for some refreshment, some chats and a few Sunday lunches for which I knew he was grateful. Just before his last club closed, I came up with an idea to put bums on seats. I would do a free cabaret, take a small percentage from the door and give that a try. It worked as far as the evening was meant to. Never had so many people been seated, as I weaved in a suit and camped and sang my way around the floor - the place buzzed. Not for long, it seemed. Financially, Laurie was not on top of his game - bankruptcy loomed. Some salvation came in the form of some buyout from another club owner Bill Gavan. Bill had taken over Laurie's previous Jug Nite Spot club site in Livery street, now called Subway City.

A few months after I had given Laurie a Sunday treat to one of Dennis's lunches and then dropped him back I received a quiet, desperate phone call from Laurie with the words, "Can you come over to me Bunny? I am dying I need to speak to you." This was completely out of character, this plea of desperation from this erstwhile formidable showman and character. I drove like a tornado and was at his house some ten minutes later. The door was open and in I walked. Laurie was seated in an armchair, a face forlorn and empty of other emotion.

"I am in terrible pain Bunn," he said, "I am on my way out. I need to sort some things out with you."

With that, I sat next to him and he told me his wishes and plans, but I was not about to accept his inevitable statement as fact. I examined him as best I could and said he must go to hospital if this pain was so severe. He decided not to go at this moment and I listened and accepted his wishes for now. He told me of his safe upstairs, gave me the combination and asked me to get his benefit each week. I went to check its contents to reassure myself that he wasn't entrusting me to lost millions. He had not. There was very little cash but a lot of cheap costume jewellery he had made himself.

As a young man he had studied costume design and become proficient at making glitter and jewels which came in very useful for his camp devotions to his subsequent Jug clubs. He was more concerned that anyone who came into the house would see these items and wanted them locked away. Amazing really that in spite of his theatricality, he was intrinsically private in such matters.

He had a neighbour who adored him and had become friendly but even she was to be similarly kept in the dark to such things. He really thought she didn't know anything about his extraordinary existence, she did of course, and I enlisted her help over the forthcoming weeks. Around five days passed and he was in no better state. I now told him I would not comply any more and phoned 999 to ensure he was taken to hospital immediately. I told them I had found him collapsed on his lounge floor, writhing in agony. A somewhat extreme description but I decided it was time for him to be investigated properly and would not back-pedal any more.

The emergency services arrived within ten minutes and I told them most truthfully that he could not walk now unaided. He was stretchered and now not protesting. He knew this was the final straw and he could not manipulate avoidance of this admission any more. It was heartbreaking to see this mini-legend carted away in such a fashion. I followed onto the ward and gave them all the information and history available to me. I knew at least that he was safer there despite my reservations of so-called modern health provision.

I visited each day for the next five days. The usual battery of tests were undertaken along with the usual assessments. It became clear that amongst a host of possible chronic health problems, kidney failure was evident. Some liver damage too was obvious and I knew he was not to make a recovery. I ensured his mind was at rest regarding his top secrets at his now locked-up house, of which I was the trusted key holder. In order to do his bidding over the next few days I fetched any items that he required.

Then I was engaged to do lectures in the south of England culminating in Taunton in Somerset for the DWP. Before leaving, it was obvious to me that Laurie by now was in a toxic confused state, becoming very quickly incoherent and disorientated. Mentioning to the staff the obvious I left telling them that I would be away for three days and I would return, they had my mobile number and were asked to keep me informed of any further deterioration. After the first day of my lecture tour I was phoned to be told of his worsened state, to be followed the following morning with the news he had died 'peacefully' that early morning. I often ask myself how we really know if death is as peaceful as it seems, but to date I can say I am not so sure or convinced.

The funeral was arranged in accordance with his wishes. Like myself, a humanist, a non-religious show was organised. I would be the officiate and relate my tales as done in this book. His departure from life's stage was related as he would have wanted. We did him proud. The crematorium was full and it truly was a celebration of this man's life. Some old chums, hardly able to shuffle through the doors, came to bid him farewell. It was a moving tribute and as I said to the assembled crowd, "You out there in the dark, all have your own stories and memories to tell. I'll tell you mine and let's compare." We did.

So much laughter prevailed as I ended the tribute with the words, "And now my ladies, let's get back to disco!" A fitting goodbye I thought. Goodbye Laurie, a dead and dying breed. He was in his mid-70s, I discovered from his hoarded documents. Bill Gaven of the Subway City club organised the funeral directors and also met the costs should any shortfall be noted in the final payment, as Laurie had not been in a position, despite his successes and failures in life, to have his final departure funded.

We are bombarded with foods we should or should not eat. How to be safe in our work place, what we must not do in so many situations. How to live our lives. The only way we can achieve this perfect world of safety is to live our life in a bubble. This would result in us suffocating to death in a hermetically-sealed environment. Getting this balance to a sensible proportion is a challenge in a modern world.

As I recall my past I recognise that I have been sometimes a great risk taker and also, where I am not so proud, I have been on occasions reckless. If I have guilt from any source, it would be from this. We can excuse it perhaps when we are young and not so informed but when we do this knowingly as adults, it is no great attribute. Some people do not take any risks if they can help it. Getting this balance is an achievement if you can manage it. I would rather have taken these risks than not. It has taught me much.

*****

November 7th 2010

I woke this morning, no it's not true I never slept at all. So many things, as we all know, run rings around a mind when still and alone. Always a little chat with Dennis as I do every day, even though I know he can never verbally answer me. I thought I had been so ill with this vile bronchitis that I couldn't go to see Isla St Clair in her mid-tours dates, this one in Monmouth. Called *'Eyes Front'* it is put together with her partner, filmmaker Patrick King. I know it's a rich tapestry of song and story with film clips, together with amusing outtakes and will make a right royal piece of entertainment. So I missed that gig but no worry, I'll see her doing her own *'Evening With'* at the Glasbury Arts Festival so we can catch up there.

It took me back to a couple of times when Dennis and I were actually doing things together now that he was less pressured. It was shortly after Larry's death. There was one occasion, when Isla invited us to Ivy Cottage in Northampton where she was living. She made it different as usual; it was a 'Murder Mystery Dinner'. Dennis naturally gravitated to the kitchen with Isla to prepare and do the food. He had bought some goodies, which he needed to prepare. Isla was busying around as we all got into our characters. I was a GP and the mystery unfolded.

Dennis never joined in the 'game', happy sitting talking with Isla AND doing his back scene routine, yet I know he thoroughly enjoyed himself. For him, he was quietly outrageous, wearing a shalwa kameez and a Turkish hat; he entered the mood, even in the kitchen. This is captured on video somewhere and only the briefest of glimpses can be seen of Dennis, sometimes puffing away at his fag.

Another time when Isla came to Vernon Cottage in Acocks Green, Alan Leighton was also joining us. Isla and her then husband had a great feast of Dennis's food delights. There was always serious talk combined with laughter. Isla would bring her guitar and do us a mini-concert after dinner with her cut-glass polished voice of traditional Scottish songs and clever ditties that I remember Larry saying, "She is truly wonderful Bunn. But I don't understand all that stuff."

Well you see it was not variety in the true sense, it's more specialist with an intellectual flavour. It's her joy and love, hence her band of admirers and newcomers to this art flock to see her in a variety of venues all over the UK. She performs unhindered by techno tricks; she has purity of voice with a wonderful warm personality.

She and Patrick came to see me shortly after I moved to the quiet of Mid Wales where I sort of settled in late 2006. Dennis would have loved their company and he is missed always at such occasions.

*****

The Black Country and its Folk

Most people know why parts of the now West Midlands was, and still is, referred to as this. Due to its heavy industrial past and its unrelenting bellowing of smoke and industrial waste - it was a grimy place. Sitting with Vivien one evening we were both reminiscing and belly laughing at some incidents and people we have encountered.

Within a community like West Bromwich, you could have people then who would never contemplate moving from some of their estates. They and the majority of their families and neighbours had lived for years, often after being resettled shortly after the war years in these burgeoning, often sprawling, communities. Between the years 1971 to nearly 1980, Vivien went to work in a doctor's practice on one of these estates. The doctor had settled and practised here from the Indian sub-continent. It was to be an amusing experience for all as it was a relatively new experience in communication and understanding for all concerned.

I will refer to one woman as Gertrude Wilson, not her real name of course. Gert was a regular visitor to the estate surgery. She was also totally unaware that her GP lived directly opposite the bingo hall. She often complained that her 'insides' had fallen out the night before. Doctor replied that they didn't seem to have fallen out when he saw her leaving the bingo hall, 'highly perfumed and lipstickated.' She was prescribed Valium which she called 'Valiant.' This was always the underlying reason for her visit.

Dialect proved to be a considerable problem in generating understanding for GPs and locums alike who found great difficulty, often impossibly, in determining the real symptoms of the patient. One evening, Vivien was working on reception when the adjoining hatch to the consulting room was flung open and she was summoned to chaperone. On entering the room she was asked, "What is this bost?" She could not stop laughing, having to compose herself and explained slowly that the patient had an abscess which was about to burst (bost).

Constipation was described as not being able to go to the ground, 'caught gooo to the grawnnd'. Respiratory problems were described as, "I cor breathe weak chest cunsumption", and menstruations often referred to as, "masturbation. I core have smear om masterbatin!" Prescriptions were called 'discriptions', periods were 'seeing' or 'flooding'. The list goes on.

Instead of a repeat prescription for Diazepam the common name known by most as Valium, "yow need to give me some more Valiant". Suspected pregnancy, "I ain't seen I think I've caught. Yow now I'm like that", with all the mime to go with it. Eye infections were, "a powke". Cystitis was "Incistitis". Coitus interruptus was described as "getting off the bus at Hill Top instead of goooin on to Carters Green". Mental illness was often referred to as, "they a right" and if someone was removed from home and taken to the psychiatric hospital, "Hers gon to the bin" or, "Hers bin put away, poor mad cow".

Sometimes, previously-issued medication that was given in the summer months was flung back through the open window, being seen as little use as they had taken it before, to the shrieks of, "Tell that bloody doctor to stick that where the sun dow shine".

Another one was a dour-looking man. Jack sat down in front of the doctor, stared him in the face and blurted, "Yow better look at me lugs. Thy am terrible".

"Ok. Stand now and pull down your trousers Jack", said the doctor taking him seriously.

"Now me lugs yow daft thing, me lugs." He meant his ears, his lug holes! Reliving this observation still has Vivien and me in stitches.

This misunderstanding of local colloquialisms and foreign understanding of more formal 'Proper English' was a comedy made in heaven. My friends Chris and Clive, in conversation, recalled when Chris's mother told him that her daughter and her husband had bought two new cars. "O really mum, what makes are they?"

"Well one is a Mini Mighty and the other is a Rover Grotesque."

If any of you recall those days, the actual cars were the Mini Maestro and the Rover Vittese. Wonderful!

Larry once said he was queuing in a post office and he heard a couple of old ladies talking solemnly about a neighbour. "Well she isn't well, she's got cancer of the Ceefax."

Once I did a show at a town called Bilston near to Wolverhampton, named The Rising Star. The audience were mainly split into two ethnicities of afro-Caribbean and Black Country folk - friends all mixing and most likely good neighbours. I would break into the Black Country lingo with a bit of stereotypical black twang. They loved it when I said to this crowd, "I had a chap once. He was good to his mother. He never went home and he was a big Jamaican lad, yow know. Big island, big heads. Not like Dominica, small island, small heads." Dressed as a mad rabbit boy it did at least add to the surreal.

Many of these overseas doctors came here, then settled and reared their families and became a big part of the community. Often their wives were horrified, thinking they were heading for the bright lights of London, Harley Street and the sophistication of the world of glamorous Britain. Little did they know what was in store for them. This was replicated all over Britain as these professionals went to all corners of the country to settle and eventually understand an English alien to them, and what a success many of them made of it. Some of these original practitioners are now well over 80.

*****

One of the things I love in life, as many of us do, is music. Listening to this is uplifting. What a voice can convey, or mood and reflection it can instil in us, whatever your generation or tastes. I remember only a few times, when performing, of having the pleasure of a five- or seven-piece band at a venue, memorable only because it never happens to lesser-knowns like myself. It's a luxury afforded to the bigger time artist, or those who can afford such production values.

I recall seeing Dorothy Squires with a 37-piece orchestra - what an amazing spectacle that was. Witnessing many times Petula Clark, now well into her 70s, and as wonderful as ever, with her arranger and musical directors. The cost for lesser mortals is prohibitive. Also, the now veteran David Essex, who I met in the 70s after a concert in Birmingham at his launch party by his then recording company CBS. He still is an amazingly skilled professional, appealing and filling concert halls successfully. His years of hard work and discipline having paid off, due to his enviable talent.

The younger artists who trudge the TV hall of fame spectacles of entertainment today and manage to get to near the final stage of the *'X Factor'* and programmes like that are eventually amazingly produced with high production cost and finance. Well I should hope so, exploitation costs a lot; besides our phone calls help fund it and the presenters' interests are paramount in the programme making. Good luck to them, the stress they go through at such a young age they deserve it. You will never see a live orchestra though.

Today for the gigging artist it's backing tracks or possibly an accompanist, like Bill Buckley was for me those years ago. Battling with your own voice is a challenge. When you do a run-through with an unknown, untried sidekick, it can be a challenge for both parties who don't know each other and styles, trends and experience can often not be compatible. Thankfully, for me, Bill was a delight. We had a few laughs, as it didn't require the voice of Pavarotti. Joe Longthorne is also a consummate and venerable professional. Get to see him if you can. Experienced, emotional and still in amazing form.

Things I don't like! Drinking out of cans. Bare light bulbs. And a filthy home. Becoming a little hard of hearing though has its compensations and large parties like weddings, preferring a funeral is for me! And those sunken lights in the ceilings - they are a pig to change when they blow. Rubbers and clips. Who invented them?

*****

Tony Carty and his partner, and also Neil and Peter. Old friends like Ken and Wendy, JB and Matt and former neighbours, many I have not mentioned, all combine to make my life richer and worthwhile. John Wood has also been a stalwart friend. That is my success, not the anonymity of a crowded dressing room full of delightful strangers, no matter how welcome. The countless students whose careers have bloomed and given them a future and the things they have also taught me. Meeting new and younger people keeps me invigorated and I hope open-minded to the new and wonderful. Having freedom and time is a great luxury and no price can be put on that. Holding on as best we can to our health without becoming too obsessive about it is a challenge once you reach the beautiful age of 60.

Two of the most important influences and loves in my life were Dennis and Larry and I enclose my own tribute to Dennis at his parting and that of Paul Vaughan, Larry's manager and agent in his later years. Paul worked hard to secure a place for Larry in the British Comedy Society, having placed a permanent plaque honouring his memory, some 12 years after his death. Situated close to the Billy Cotton plaque of the Shepherds Bush Empire, that Larry was so fond of. Paul's invite to me on that day saw me cutting a trip short from West Africa to be there. I would not have missed it for any amount of world travel. Home is where the heart is and the good memories.

It was unveiled by Sir Terry Wogan on the 30th May 2006 with the adage from Paul, "As you know, Larry held you in such highest esteem." This means so much to me. At that event were many luminaries and for a while, posing for a picture with Norman Wisdom, you could see this old professional actor swing into a pose as easy as him tripping on the floor. Aware of any camera, he was in full flight and ready to perform at 90 years of age, now sadly gone.

The speech given by Paul Vaughan at the Kensington Hilton Hotel 30th May 2006:

"Chairman and officers of the British Comedy Society, Knights of the Realm, Dame Dora Bryan (of whom Larry always said, 'If she isn't yet, she jolly well ought to be!'), distinguished guests, eminent former colleagues, friends and admirers of Larry Grayson all.

It would have assuredly have gladdened Larry's heart to know that he was being remembered and honoured today and by such a richly diverse company.

Although he grew up and later worked in an era in which any show of sentiment was widely held to be a form of weakness - the stiff upper lip being rather the accepted order in those days - with Larry, a rich and genuine seam of emotion ran close to the surface. And when, perhaps unfashionably but always unfailingly at the end of every show, be it stage or television he addressed his audience and said:

'Goodnight, God Bless and I love you very much.' These were the feelings of utmost honesty that flowed straight from his heart, a direct response he said to the waves of love that he felt pouring towards him from the footlights wherever he went. Larry Grayson was a very loveable man.

There was another side to Larry, one that bore testament to a deeply rooted resilience, determination and grit. As many of us know, he was fostered into a family for which love, warmth, care and respect for others, solid morals and a quiet but devout belief in Almighty God were the deeply etched hallmarks.

From an early age, his incisive eye and perceptive ear provided him with a treasure chest of material, much of it based on the conversations of those around him, notably his foster parents' daughters, May and his beloved Flo, always known as Fan, to whom ultimately fell the task, a task which she carried out selflessly and in an exemplary manner, of bringing him up.

One day, he and his young school chums fell in to discussing their futures in a corner of the playground. There were the inevitable would-be engine drivers, shopkeepers and those that knew, come what may, they were going to follow their dads down the pit.

'And what are you going to be?' they asked Larry. Without a beat of hesitation he replied, 'I am going to be a star.'

The cruel howls of derision could be heard a mile away. One little inquisitor - perhaps with lawyer printed all over him asked him sneeringly, 'Can you sing?'

'No.' said Larry.

'Can you dance?'

'No.' replied Larry.

'Can you play the piano?'

'No,' admitted Larry, 'but I am still going to be a star! So there!'

It was that never-faltering resilience and determination that was to carry him to the top of the tree. All through his professional life, which began at the age of fourteen in the Fife Street Working Men's Club, he never failed to do his best, honing his craft and polishing his timing, in theatres and other venues up and down the land, no matter the size or importance of the platform, often being obliged to compete, as so were many others, with wilfully oblivious waitresses bearing slopping trays of ale and chicken in the basket.

He also painted a picture for us, as only he could, of the inevitable kiddies' wet Wednesday afternoon pantos, at which - so he told us graphically - from the moment the curtain went up, the all-pervading aroma was of excited wee - wee and oranges. These were, he said, equally as important as the big Saturday night performances. And you never knew when the likes of Billy Marsh were hovering at the back of the stalls looking to promote only the very best of what was on stage, to the honour of Moss Empires touring perhaps.

Larry never failed to be amazed and inordinately grateful for the good fortune that translated him from the back street of Nuneaton and brought him to work with some of the great names behind as well as in front of the camera.

He never forgot his debt to Joe (Will) Collins and Eve Taylor or Michael, Leslie and Lew Grade who launched him and his chair on an unsuspecting viewing public on ATV's smash hit *'Saturday Night Variety'*.

But Fan was always there, ready to welcome him home, not only looking after him as she had always done, but never failing, even when he was a household name, to keep his feet firmly on the ground.

In 1972, to his considerable amazement, Larry was to top the bill at what he always called 'The Vatican of Show Business', the world famous London Palladium which occupies the block cornered by Argyll Street and Great Marlborough Street. The little lad from Nuneaton had achieved the impossible, even in his eyes.

In London for the preliminary discussions and costume fittings, he rang Fan from a telephone box in Great Marlborough Street.

'Fan...' he said after he had pressed button A. 'Fan. You won't believe it. I am here in London in a phone box, opposite the London Palladium.'

'That's nice.' said Fan.

'And...' a wave of true emotion began to surface and his voice began to falter, 'There's a huge poster, Fan, all across the theatre. It's ever so big and it's all lit up, you cant miss it. And oh Fan, my name is above the title in the biggest letters ever. It says *'Larry Grayson, in Grayson's Scandals'*. Oh Fan!'

'Yes that's very well,' replied Fan, 'but the coalman's just been. Do we want two bags or three?'

But his loving respect for Fan was absolute and he never forgot the debt he owed her. Wherever he was he would ring her every day and would often pop out saying, 'I must just get something for the little lady.'

And his regard for Alan Boyd - who, with Bill Cotton and Jim Moir, bravely but perceptively cast him from what must have been a long list, thus creating *'Larry Grayson's Generation Game'* - was considerable, as it was for the team that the BBC then gathered around him, Marcus Plantin, Paul Jackson, Bill Morton and Ronnie Hazlehurst to name but a few. And also for his good friend Kevin Bishop who presciently booked him and steered him, only a few weeks before his death, through his spot on the *'Royal Variety Performance'* in the presence of her late Majesty Queen Elizabeth the Queen Mother. Although none of us knew it then, it was to be his last ever public appearance.

And while on matters royal, may I say what a pleasure it is to welcome here today another of Larry's good friends, her late Majesty's former steward, Mr William Tallon who attended Larry's memorial service in St Paul's, Covent Garden, charged with reporting every last detail back to Clarence House!

And Larry's respect for what he called, 'the gods of the sixth floor' was absolute too. Whenever invited to their presence at Television Centre, he was genuinely and perhaps endearingly nervous. So I know that he would want me to thank Sir Bill Cotton and Jim Moir for paying him the great compliment of being here today.

Although it is now more than eleven years since Larry Grayson died - on the seventh of January, 1995, I also know that he would have been gratefully moved, perhaps even to tears, by the honour done to him today by his old friend Sir Terry Wogan and the British Comedy Society, and by all those who are remembering him. However, rather as he reacted to his arrival at the top of the show business tree somewhat late in life, I think he might have added with a measure of mischief, 'What kept you?'

And while I am on the subject, forgive me if I raise a surprised eyebrow (or even two) that, even after all this time, Nuneaton, the town which he loved and the town in which he chose to die, and a town which he helped to put on a wider map, has never done him the honour of remembering him with so much as a park bench or a flower bed.

'Not quite the sort of person we want to honour.' I once heard reported as a comment alleged to have emanated from the Town Hall when, some years ago, the matter was discussed.

Clearly, today and thank heavens for it, times are at last beginning to change, and while his memorial plaque might bear his catchphrase, 'Shut That Door', it is ironic is it not that, in truth, and perhaps without even realising it, he did so much to open so many doors and to allow a welcome breeze to begin to blow away some at least of the cobwebs of bigotry and obfuscation.

A short while ago, over on the other side of the Green, at the former BBC Television Centre (which Larry revered as he did the dear old Shepherds Bush Empire), home over the years to so many great stars and to many milestones in broadcasting history, I was thinking back as I often do to the happy times we all enjoyed there. Larry and Isla, another fine example of BBC casting, in the midst of so many guests and the celebrities who, week by week, willingly and gladly came to pop through *'Larry's Generation Game'* doors, thus bringing surprised delight not only to him but also of course to the BBC's massive Saturday night television audience. They were, he said later, some of the happiest days of his life.

Little did any of us think then that, close on three decades later, thanks to the initiative of the British Comedy Society (for which we all thank them warmly), we survivors, as is our privilege today, would gather back in Shepherds Bush to pay tribute to a dear man of honesty and integrity, who gave us the gift of his friendship, who never failed to make us laugh, privately or publicly, a performer of considerable talent whose determination and resilience in the face of so many odds has always been, and I pray will forever continue to be, a inspiration and example to us all.

Dear Larry - As we drove around the country (and if possible never on the motorways) you never missed an opportunity to pop into little village churches, for a few moments of peace and quiet. And, ever curious, you always wanted to know the meanings of the inscriptions and Latin mottos that adorned the tombs and effigies. So try this for size!

Si monumentum requires, circumspice.

If you are seeking your memorial, look around you.

You may be gone, but you have not been forgotten."

What a tribute Paul, one never to be forgotten.

I was able to also give my own small contribution publicly at The Larry Grayson Memorial Concert at the Bedworth Civic Hall on Wednesday 3rd May, 1995, where I was billed and introduced onto the stage by the lovely Isla St Clair on the bill as 'Bunny Thomas, zany comedian, friend and admirer of Larry's!'

I was naughty, camped it up, sang a number and left the stage in tears saying to the crowd, "Goodnight Larry I love you very much." Those words he used himself at the end of his own wonderful shows. The proceeds of this concert, produced by Brian Walker were targeted for the Friends of the George Eliot CT Scanner Appeal. Over the next few years I always included a question and answer session in the shows where I was often asked about him. I did and also gave tribute to Larry at every opportunity.

*****

CHAPTER 17
YOURS UNTIL THE LIMELIGHT FADES. ONE OF MANY FINAL CURTAINS.

Now for Dennis.

I engaged a humanist officiant named Brian Hill, a good man who explained to the assembled crowd about the philosophy of humanism, and that this was Dennis's wish and choice. It was a celebration of life lived and our attempt to say goodbye in our own way and should anyone wish to use their faith at the end to say private prayer if they wish. As this was a non-religious ceremony it was, as in all ceremonies of this nature, a time to reflect on our own experiences of him, be them whatever.

As humanists believe that we all can have a good moral life, without the belief in a creator, they also believe the individual's rights to freedom and choice in the main decisions affecting each life and death. They believe that all people are of equal worth, regardless of gender, culture, race, age, sexual orientation or ability. Any pain that we may have had in life is now gone forever.

My part in this is as follows:

> "Life is that thing that happens to us all while we are planning to do something else! And they say you never truly appreciate something or know what you have until you lose it.
>
> Well I always knew what I had well before I lost it, in Dennis, my long-term companion for over 35 years. Life teaches some of us many things, and others it teaches nothing because they are unable to change because of it. Dennis truly changed me, not to the outside world, but my inner life that made me richer and wiser from knowing him.
>
> Others see a relationship between two parties in many ways - he was off-hand, he was crusty, fearful, riddled with doubt, solitary, patient, selfless, funny, sarcastic, sad, happy, lonely, or just successful. Difficult, devoted, unselfish, foolish, naive. Only the two of you truly know. I knew Dennis and he knew me. We accepted each other for what we were, we never lied or

cheated on each other, in the full knowledge of what pain may be caused. I conducted my life with him as honestly as I could and he asked nothing in return.

He accepted me unconditionally, wholeheartedly in the knowledge of who I am.

Life often cracked his heart, but as weak as he may have seemed, he was stronger than the Rock of Gibraltar, as solid and as dependable as the rain and the sun, he was my existence. He truly was my love. He had choices like us all and he chose to stay in my life even when I pained him. He always wanted for my happiness, often at the expense of his own. He needed and wanted no one else.

In his early life, he survived the equivalent of an emotional holocaust. It damaged him for later life, yet even when his body and mind cracking under its weight, he had a strength of unimaginable proportions. Dennis always did what he wanted in the full knowledge of where it may lead him.

He seemed a simple man, he always said he was, yet he demonstrated amazing skill leading him to enduring success and creativity. He had great stature. We are always expected to speak well of the dead, but I truly can. If others sometimes gave me comfort, he gave me loyalty and love, more than ever they could. If I was hurt, he was hurt.

Damaged from an early age at the hands of cruel and wicked people where he was abandoned as a baby, given into the care of a system riddled with inadequacies, he learned to get up and get on with it. He knew he was on his own. He had his fun as a very young man, as we all did, yet he allowed me to take his life and mend it, in the full knowledge of my nagging and persistence and eccentricities and often extremes, which were a strange comfort to him, telling him he was safe and loved, from a world he knew was far from perfect.

He was kind and accepting of others. I believe he never truly did any lasting damage or harm to anyone. He accepted my often strange and theatrical and professional life with a knowing tongue in his cheek, and provided all he could for me with no fuss or ceremony all his life. Well I did often tell him I was the illegitimate child of Princess Margaret!

In his darkest hours he knew he could rely on me when others may have doubted my persistence. I did what had to be done. I kept my promise to him. I took him home from a good place to a better place to die, in a room he always wanted - to share with the person he loved - he chose me, what can be more fulfilling than that? As I age and learn, he has taught me more about myself than all my intellectual capabilities, my knowledge of psychiatry and so-called clever works of mankind. He was my education - he was my life and as it continues, I will manage it in sadness and in memory of him and will do better because of knowing him.

He will be with me till the end, and I am a happy man."

That was it, brief yet to the point, said with all the passion I had inside and I meant each and every word as I lived it. Amazingly, I was not to spend hours working this out, I left it till very near the day and Vivien was staying over in the top bedroom. As usual, I couldn't sleep and this amazing energy came over me at 3am and I shot out of bed to the writing pad and it just flowed from me and I don't know where from, I then darted in to Viv, woke her up from slumber to pronounce, "I have done it". "Mad cow", she must have thought.

It was done so quickly and as I spoke these words that day in January the sun shone through and many a tear and smile was shed for him, and reliving this now in words once more it's forever with me. It's amazing too that just one decade apart on the same date both Dennis and Larry died on the 7th January.

*****

Sadly gone. My Dennis, never forgotten.

Bunny Thomas, doing what I do best.

Why the title of this book? I was reminded of those more innocent times by Vivien and Gordon, just recently. Gordon was fortunate to have been doted on by his mother and, being fatherless, also a maiden aunt. Due to this they always spoiled him and as a very young man from earlier than 17 he always had a car, shiny and polished, no doubt its funding assisted by these adoring ladies. He had some beauties: a Consul, a Zephyr and also a large Zodiac, a very American design for its time as well as others. These versions were mid 60s and it was now 1967.

That night we went cruising out of West Bromwich district as we did as often as we could, driving to the nearest, more countrified areas out of Dudley and towards the Kidderminster areas. One night, I insisted we pulled in for a drink in a place named Wall Heath. I think the name of this pub was like a million others, the Old Wagon and Horse. It was very charming. I recall that it was just 10.30 pm as we raced to the door to be met by the landlady. "Sorry Darling. It's Way Past Time." It was just minutes after 10.30. How times have moved on. She was blonde, glam and such a Bet Lynch-type character, with her waving hands and gestures and the drawl was something so memorable and camp - just like a *'Carry On'* scene. Well, when you realise that it was not uncommon for the police to arrive at pubs a few minutes after closing time and caution them if they were outside the licensing hours. Well I am sorry for many things and its never way past time to say or admit it.

Sarah-Jane Sikora, in many conversations, said I should do this, so blame her that I did.

In September 2009 she asked me to do a comedy auction at one of her gallery exhibitions in Cork Street in the West End. I duly obliged and we raised quite a few thousand pounds for the Alzheimer's Society. She also sold most of her original paintings to boot, so all were happy to see those crowds smiling at her talent and collecting her work gave me hope and joy. To have known great talents past and present has made me happy. To have been present and a part of the developments in psychiatry and mental health has kept my eyes open to a changing, ever remarkable world. To have shared a good chunk of my life with Dennis has made it all worthwhile and I hope there is much more to this story rather than a finale. For me it's yet another beginning. Thank you for sharing this with me.